ACCLAIM FOR Siobhan Darrow's

Flirting with Danger

"Siobhan Darrow finally awards us with the one story which we haven't yet read: *Flirting with Danger* is not another tale told by a gutsy female war correspondent set out to impress us and make us feel like wimps, but the disarmingly honest story of a woman who manages to keep her set of values and priorities straight, while wading through warfare, stormy love affairs and a glamorous career in journalism . . . without ever leaving her humor behind."
—Francesca Marciano, author of *Rules of the Wild*

"A brave and exciting piece of writing."   —*Image* magazine

"As one of CNN's star reporters, Darrow's seen more hot spots . . . The Russian uprising, civil wars in Georgia and Chechnya, Princess Di's funeral, Northern Ireland—she covered them all."
—*Sunday Herald*

"Siobhan Darrow grew up on food stamps, became a war reporter and covered the globe, always in love (she dumped Ted Turner!), bearing witness to the last decade's defining moments. She writes of Georgian rebels serving a eight-course feast in the middle of battle, of Chechen soldiers and spitting roosters, with equal warmth. This is a lovely book."   —Matt Klam, author of *Sam the Cat*

D0089918

"Terrific . . . An instructive story of one woman's rise to a dream job in a tough profession, a revealing insider's view of modern warfare and the one-sided video journalism that brings it to our living rooms, and the candid account of a woman intensely living, working, and loving in a post-feminist world of choice—inventing and reinventing her life. Brave, smart, wry, and deeply thoughtful, Siobhan Darrow is a woman to read and reckon with."

—Ann Jones, author of *Looking for Lovedu*

"Everyone knows about Christiane Amanpour, but fellow CNN reporter Siobhan Darrow has also had her moments. *Flirting with Danger* takes us from Belfast (where she was born) to Russia (where she became a 'Cold War bride') and the dangerous places she visited as a top TV jounalist." —*Condé Nast Traveller* (Europe)

Siobhan Darrow

Flirting with Danger

Siobhan Darrow has worked for CNN for nearly fifteen years, serving as a correspondent in Russia, Great Britain, Northern Ireland, the Balkans, Israel, Chechnya, and Albania.

Flirting with Danger

Flirting with Danger

Confessions of

a Reluctant War Reporter

Siobhan Darrow

ANCHOR BOOKS

A Division of Random House, Inc.

New York

AN ANCHOR ORIGINAL, JANUARY 2002

Library of Congress Cataloging-in-Publication Data

Darrow, Siobhan.
Flirting with danger : confessions of a reluctant war reporter /
Siobhan Darrow.
p.   cm.
ISBN 0-385-72134-X
1. Darrow, Siobhan. 2. War correspondents—United States—
Biography. 3. Foreign correspondents—United States—Biography.
1. Title.
PN4874.D354 A3   2002
070.4'333'092—dc21
[B]
2001045102

Anchor ISBN: 0-385-72134-X

Book design by Mia Risberg

www.anchorbooks.com

Printed in the United States of America
10   9   8   7   6   5   4   3   2   1

To Shep, for finding me

Contents

Flirting with Danger

Animal Sanctuary

Joy usually entered our house on four legs, sometimes on two webbed feet or a pair of wings. When I was growing up, no matter how little money we had, there always seemed to be enough to feed another tiny amphibian, canine, or feline mouth. My mother loved animals, and I think having them around helped keep her sane. There was Lion Face, the big orange tomcat who fathered innumerable kittens. There were the African frogs, who accidentally froze on the windowsill one sudden winter's day, their limbs captured midstroke, trapped in an icy grave. And there were the gerbils I won at school by guessing how many beans were in a jar. My cat ate them and left their carcasses on my pillow—her pillow. Perhaps it was an innocent offering, or maybe a warning not to betray her with other animals. I accepted the violence in my animal world. It had rumbled around my human world ever since I can remember.

I was born in Belfast, Northern Ireland. I lived with my grandparents, my older sister, Alexandra, and my mother during one of our many separations from my American father. My grandfather always sat in his wheelchair by the fireplace; one of his legs had been shot off in the First World War. In our bedroom, an old grenade lay on the mantel piece, a daily reminder of the danger lurking outside. The "Troubles," as people in Northern Ireland called their bloodshed, were still brewing but had not fully erupted yet. It was 1963. When we crossed the ocean to America, turmoil came with us and took root in our home in New Jersey. I found sanctuary with the animals.

When we got a dark Siamese cat, my mother said I could name her. I was paralyzed with indecision. "How about Lap Sang or Soo Chong?" my mother offered, referring to the names of Oriental teas. I was too excited to choose, so we combined them into Lap Sue. I hoped that since I had named her, she would be mine. As it turned out, nobody else could stand her. She could be vicious, clawing and scratching anyone who went near her, but I loved her. I tried to stay on her good side, giving her my pillow each night, and when her long feline limbs sprawled across it as if it were her throne, I craned and twisted my neck to the side so as not to disturb her. Once Lap Sue savaged the leg of a visiting child so badly the girl needed stitches, and I was terrified her mother would demand the cat be put to death and I would lose her. My mother defended Lap Sue valiantly. I wished that she would defend me the same way. When my mother had something to express to me, she directed it at Lap Sue. In our house, humans were discouraged from showing emotions. Instead, we learned to show our feelings with the animals.

I relied on Lap Sue. She purred so loudly that when I curled up and laid my head against the soft fur of her belly, her inner motor drowned out the yelling. It would start when my father came home.

It was usually late and we would be in our bunk beds. Alexandra was on the bottom; Lap Sue and I were on the top. I'd stroke her silky body and stare into her pale blue eyes. She'd stare back, half squinting, her eyes reassuring me. I would lie quietly, my body tensed, hearing but not wanting to hear, knowing I had to listen to make sure nothing bad happened, to make sure my mother was OK. I would creep out of bed and crack open the door. "Go back to your room," she'd say. "I'm fine."

One of my clearest early memories is of a summer's day when a whale washed ashore at the beach. It was my first contact with the world that would one day dominate my life: television. I was six, Alexandra was seven, and our baby sister, Francesca, was two. We were in Kennebunkport, Maine. It was a treat to trade New Jersey's sweltering summer heat for the cooler New England beach. Even rarer, we were all together, a mother and father and three little girls with sand pails and bathing suits, staying in a motel room with a kitchenette, on a real family vacation. Some nights we got to eat dinner out, with the thrill of grilled cheese and French fries, which we never had at home. Other nights my mother cooked fresh seafood, including lobsters. We made friends with the crustaceans en route from the fish market, and when they were lowered into their liquid graves, the cauldron of boiling water on the stove, it broke our hearts. During the days, we frolicked in the giant waves of the Atlantic. My parents were born on either side of this ocean, and by now the gulf between them had grown as wide and as deep. The beach was my father's domain; my mother's fair skin kept her out of the sun, so it was my father who played with us by the sea. Out in the waves, he held us tight so we wouldn't go under. We squealed in delight.

One morning the tranquil scene was spoiled. Surrounded by a gathering crowd, an enormous gray blob was lying on the beach. At first I could not figure out what it was. I had never seen anything like it. It was giant and smelled sickly, choking the freshness of the sea air. A moat of gooey oil streaked with blood surrounded it. Finally I understood that it was a baby whale that had been hit by a boat, its big blubbery corpse now washed up on the beach. Soon a local TV reporter arrived. It was the first time I had ever seen a TV camera. The crew filmed the giant ocean casualty and then turned their camera on me. Now I realize what a perfect television image it was, a small girl weeping at the sight of this huge, wasteful death. Later, viewing the world's pain through a TV lens became my way of life.

My mother was Scots-Irish, from a well-to-do Protestant family in Belfast, Northern Ireland, the daughter of a barrister with a houseful of servants. My father was the son of an overbearing immigrant Jewish mother who landed in New Jersey and burdened her children with all the pain and paranoia of the small Russian village she grew up in. When my parents met at medical school in Belfast, their romance spoiled each other's plans to be a doctor. Years later I came to see what an act of rebellion their union was for each of them. For my father, my mother's proper British ways were a distinct step outside the insular family life of Jewish immigrants whose ambition—to turn their son into a doctor—was more important than love or happiness. For my mother, befriending a clever and charming American was an escape from the cloistered life of postwar Northern Ireland. They married quickly, and Alexandra and I were born within a couple of years. My mother quit medical school to take care of us. My father was unable to finish either, and was reduced to taking odd jobs.

By the time we moved to America in 1964, there was already

tumult in my parents' domestic life. My father had been so afraid of his domineering family that he could not bring himself to tell his own mother that he had married a non-Jew. He didn't tell her that he was married at all, or that her first grandchildren had been born. When he went home to New Jersey, ahead of us, he still did not tell his family. No doubt he was afraid that his mother would blame his failure at medical school on this Protestant woman, this shiksa who had lured him into marriage.

When my mother, Alexandra, and I arrived by ship, he met us at the pier. But there was no home to go to. For a while we lived like vagabonds, traipsing from the house of one acquaintance to the next. Once he finally confessed to our existence, my father's mother and sister refused to see us. They wielded enough emotional power over him to make him unwilling or unable to stand up to them, and he often went to see them by himself.

Although I never really got to know him, relatives told me later that my father was a highly intelligent and emotional man who had trouble holding a job for long. Most of what money he did earn went to his mother, so deep was his guilt about marrying outside the tribe. As a result, his wife was essentially stranded in a foreign land with small children she could barely feed. As we grew up, we lived a half hour away from my grandmother, but she still would not see us, her only grandchildren.

Uncle Leon, my father's unmarried older brother, was the only member of his family who broke ranks and came to visit. He had no wife or children of his own and lived with my grandmother, so we were the closest he ever got to a taste of family life. He probably braved a lot of wrath from his mother by coming to see us, but he came anyway. He was the only connection I had to my father's family.

As a child, I worshiped my mother. She was beautiful, strong, and regal, despite the decidedly unregal circumstances in which we often lived. She held her head high in a town where people were generally judged by their income. Perhaps she was spared harsh judgment because she was an outsider and appeared sophisticated even while lugging our dirty clothes to the Laundromat or paying for our groceries with food stamps. I knew how badly we needed the government-sponsored food aid, but I was embarrassed when she pulled out the blue-and-green booklet while we were standing in the supermarket line, wishing she would take them out at the last minute so nobody but the checkout person would see. With this shame, I often weighed whether or not to go to the supermarket with her, but my desire to be with her usually won out. She was devoted to us, and we to her. She worked three jobs to pay for our ballet classes and my oboe lessons. After all she sacrificed, I was terrified of failing her by bringing home a bad report card. She was a firm disciplinarian, determined to see us work hard. She always corrected our grammar, forbade gum chewing, and hounded us to do our homework. I could always get out of doing menial tasks like the dishes if I went and practiced my oboe.

My mother never let our poverty define us. With whatever she had, she always bought the best. We ate Swiss chocolates or none at all. She concocted exquisite meals on our food-stamp fare. It didn't matter how tatty our apartment was; it was often full of distinguished academics from a nearby university who, oblivious to the surroundings, were drawn to my mother's charm, beauty, and excellent cooking. My mother felt superior to most Americans: she thought American wealth was vulgar, so often unaccompanied by good manners, education, or social refinement. She had nothing but contempt for the parents of my more affluent friends, whose children would go home to an empty house and whose mothers took them to McDonald's. We often had no money for new school clothes but were brought up to believe we were somehow better bred than the other children.

Having been brought up with servants, my mother wasn't born to housework. She always seemed to be ironing or sorting clothes, but despite her valiant attempts, our house always looked like a mess. There were mountains of laundry, piles of dishes, stacks of books. And the newspapers. They were everywhere. My father collected them and refused to let my mother throw them out. They lined the walls of my parents' bedroom, yellow, dusty, and half-read. The electricity and phone were often turned off because my father had not given her money to pay the bills, but our sheets were ironed meticulously, as were the linen napkins. Perhaps it soothed her to make some order in the chaos that she fought so hard to hide.

To my mother, expressing an emotion was a bad American habit to be discouraged. "It's vulgar to talk about yourself," she would often say, though sometimes she talked of the grand life she had left behind in Belfast. I loved hearing her stories, partly because her life seemed such a mystery. She had lived in the country with horses and dogs. It seemed a lot to give up to be with us. I often feared that she'd tire of our life and go back to her exalted country, leaving us behind. I wanted to be good and not let her down, to give her every reason to stay. I stuck to her side like glue, terrified to let her out of my sight. Many years later, I thought that maybe because I spent so much time keeping track of her, somewhere along the way I lost track of myself.

I learned to subsist on tiny crumbs of love. My mother was an extraordinary cook, but emotional sustenance was scarce. It must have taken all her strength to hunker down and survive and bring us up practically on her own. Maybe she couldn't let down her reserve, even for a minute, for fear it would all unravel. She seemed to pour all her love into feeding us elaborately. But I still felt emotionally malnourished. I learned to sate my hunger in unsavory places later on, with men so incapable of showing affection that they always left me in a state of near-starvation. I thought it was like indulging in fast food: when you eat greasy French fries, you know you'll regret it later. But sometimes I was so ravenous I didn't care. I seemed to accept almost any man who took notice and paid attention to me. I often failed to look them over and see how unappetizing they were. Always so well fed, yet starving.

Since my father wasn't around much, I lived in an all-female world with my mother and two sisters. My towering flame-haired mother with her long, chiseled, aristocratic nose looked as if she had stepped out of the Victorian era. Alexandra looked wild and woolly, with an exquisite face that also looked as if it were from an earlier century, a face more at home on the walls of Europe's finest art galleries than the streets of New Jersey. I, too, had corkscrew-curly hair, and no amount of ironing or hair rollers would straighten it enough to let me look like my classmates. Francesca, the youngest, with straight blond hair and huge blue eyes, always seemed the most American. We used to call her Marilyn, from *The Munsters,* that seventies TV show about a family of assorted freaks and vampires that had one normal-looking relative.

The three of us loved to compare body parts with my mother's. Who looked most like her was a favorite topic of conversation, and whoever had more in common with her felt most loved. My hands and feet were identical to hers, which somehow assured me a permanent connection to her. Any feature attributed to my father was construed as an insult and major structural flaw. Not that his six-foot-plus frame, pale curls, and hazel eyes should have been a source of shame. According to my mother, Francesca and I seemed to have been cloned from her, while she would tell my older sister, Alexandra, that she was my father's spitting image, piercing Alexandra's self-esteem. Sometimes I ventured that my green eyes and curly hair might have come from his side of the gene pool, but my mother always insisted, despite her straight hair, that my curls came from her side, since her brother had curly hair. It was easier for me to agree than to make any case at all for my father. He was the bad guy, and showing him any sympathy was more trouble than it was worth. Many years later I learned that it works the same way in any war: those who can see both sides eventually learn to keep quiet. So I kept to myself what sympathies I had for my father, like my secret love of kosher dill pickles. Occasionally I could see how he wanted to be part of us. But mostly I just wished he would go away and leave us in peace.

We treated my father as an alien invader. His presence, perhaps because it was infrequent, was always an intrusion. When he walked through the front door, I knew it meant trouble. Siding with my mother, I saw him as the bully who came into our lives and trampled on our daily rituals. My mother brought us up with a mixture of aristocratic tastes and sensibilities and disdain for money. She always stressed the importance of maintaining standards, from good school grades to proper table manners. We were taught to use a saucer with our teacups, and she would bake homemade éclairs for our afternoon tea. My father would turn up and plop himself down at the table with his shirt out and the top button of his pants undone and dive into a box of cornflakes. My mother would watch in disgust with me at her side, a loyal deputy, as he sliced bananas into bowl after bowl of cereal. It was a cultural feud. He wasn't one of us. The tension led to a perpetual state of warfare in our home. It vacillated from the cold-war variety of icy, disapproving stares to sudden explosions of violence.

When we were growing up, I never understood why my father often disappeared for days at a time. Sometimes he would say he was going out to the market to get milk on a Friday night, and not show up at home until Sunday night. Only later did I realize that he was slinking off to spend the weekend with his mother and sister. Torn between two families, he was destined to disappoint both.

By the time I was a teenager, I too lived a double life. I ignored the anger and despair that shrouded nearly every exchange between my parents. I did my homework and brought home my honor-society grades. I played in the school band and acted in school plays. I seemed quiet and good but I was beginning to be someone else. I smoked dope with my friends and puffed on cigarettes under the bleachers on the football field. With my mature looks and buxom figure, I could buy booze and not be asked to show ID. I took to shoplifting, both stealing and also using a price-changing technique of peeling off the sticker and putting a cheaper tag on my target. Perhaps it was inevitable that I would get caught.

One day the store buzzer rang as Cindy, my best friend of the week, and I stepped out the door of Bamberger's. Beach season was approaching, and my part-time-waitress wages at Dunkin' Donuts were not enough to get the right clothes. The two new bathing suits I had carefully hidden under my shirt must have had some new secret device that eluded my notice. The store security guard hauled us back inside and marched us to an office while he called the police. "They are just trying to scare us," I told Cindy, a novice at theft compared with me. But before long we were in the backseat of a squad car, in handcuffs, two fifteen-year-old girls. I tried to make light of it, joking to Cindy, "If we were going to get caught, we should have at least ripped off Saks."

The store security's call to the police was one thing. But the police did something a hundred times worse: they called our parents. Cindy was crying. I was still trying to make her laugh, although I knew I was in big trouble. I hated disappointing my mother. The police let me off easy. I had to write an essay on why it is wrong to steal. I learned my first lesson on writing one's way through the chaos inside. I also learned that I was comfortable living on the edge.

My mother let me off easy too. She was distracted by larger problems. She didn't tell my father about the incident, sparing him the worry. A medical checkup for a new job he had landed detected swollen lymph glands. I didn't really understand what that meant, but no one discussed it. Alexandra and I, through overheard snatches of conversation and by trading intelligence, became vaguely aware of my parents' anxiety over medical insurance and whether my father would get it before his new employers realized he had cancer. I tried to ignore the medicine cabinet that was suddenly overflowing with drugs to kill my father's cancer, and more drugs to kill the side effects.

That summer I went away to Barbados after being selected as an American Field Service exchange student. My father wanted to take me shopping for new summer dresses before I left. I felt awkward about going with him, but he insisted. When he decided we'd go to Bambergers, I was terrified that the store security would recognize me and toss us out. They didn't. My father helped me choose a few cotton shifts for my big adventure. There was a brown-and-white-striped dress he particularly liked. I didn't, but I took it anyway to please him. It was one of only a handful of intimate memories I have of us together as father and daughter. With death looming, he was trying to get to know the daughters whose childhood he missed.

Although I was still only a teenager, I learned the art of escape through travel. I wanted to get as far away as possible from my life in Highland Park, New Jersey. I had been chosen to represent my high school after a series of interviews with community members and teachers whom I convinced of my ability to adjust to a new country. It made sense: a clash of cultures had been under way in my own home since I was an infant. Two alien cultures lived under one roof with no dialogue, just hostility, misunderstanding, and resentment. I'd been straddling the customs of two worlds all my life.

It was the mid-seventies when I left for Barbados. There had been race riots in New Jersey and all over America, giving me a sense of looming crisis. But suddenly I was living with all black people, in a calm and peaceful environment. Now it was my turn to feel what it was like to be the outsider, to be the one in the minority. Sometimes it made me uncomfortable, but people in Barbados are so friendly, most of the time my racial differences were cause for laughter. When I first arrived at the home of my host sister, Janice, her five-year-old nephew walked into a bedroom where I sat, and he ran away screaming. "There's a big white doll in Janice's room!" After I was settled in and started to forget about race, I was walking downtown with Janice and a bunch of her friends one day when I caught a glimpse of us in a shop window. It took me by surprise to see how much I stood out. Janice and I came from completely different worlds, yet as teenagers we found it easy to understand each other. She'd cornrow my curly blond hair just like her other friends'. We often hit the discos, or cut school to hang around downtown, checking out the boys. West Indians have a penchant for standing around on street corners, gabbing and watching the world go by. They called it liming. It was good training for all those future stakeouts I had to endure as a reporter, waiting around for hours for faceless officials to emerge from a meeting. For Janice, who dreamed of getting off that tiny island one day, I seemed an emissary from another world. For me, this lush tropical paradise let me forget the world I'd left.

But my refuge was cut short. When my father was taken to the hospital, my mother called to tell me to come home. I said good-bye to Janice, not knowing it would be more than two decades before our next meeting. I landed at JFK Airport, and Alexandra, at seventeen, just old enough for a new driver's license, was sent to get me. She had been warned not to tell me until we got home. But when I asked her if we were going directly to the hospital, she let it out. Somewhere between the Brooklyn Queens Expressway and the New Jersey Turnpike, Alexandra told me that I wouldn't see my father again. He had died a few hours before my plane landed. All those years as a small girl, I had hoped my father would somehow leave our lives. I never imagined he would do it by dying.

My mother told me later that she had decided not to tell me how ill my father was, justifying it by saying she didn't want to ruin my big trip. But I always wished she had. I needed to see him one more time, to say good-bye. My mother had indirectly trained me not to like my father and to reject him, so I didn't know what to feel about losing him. I repressed the pain and confusion, allowing it to fester for years.

His funeral is a blur in my mind. I arrived at the last minute, so there was no time or perspective to absorb it. I wasn't prepared at all. Jet travel allows no time for adjustment. One minute I was drinking rum on the beach in Barbados, the next burying my father in New Jersey. I remember being ashamed of his plain, unvarnished coffin. I thought it was the final indignity of our poverty. I learned later that it was what he wanted. A simple coffin is part of the Jewish faith. A rabbi performed the ceremony at the funeral home as a courtesy to my Protestant mother, who had better ties to the Jewish community than my father did. He wasn't a member, so the service couldn't take place at the temple. Despite her anger with my father, my mother had a deep respect for Judiasm and scraped together a minyan, the required ten Jewish men, to carry the coffin, carrying out my father's wishes to the letter. I wore the brown-and-white dress we had picked out together before I left for Barbados.

My last year in high school was unhappy. My insides felt gouged out by my father's death, and the ensuing instability in our home made it worse. I started reading *The New York Times,* which my mother revered, and I began to focus my anxiety on the outside world. It was 1976, and the stories about the Soviet Union and arms control grabbed my attention. I became terrified by the possibility of a nuclear war. During loud storms in the middle of the night, I sometimes awoke with a start, convinced the end had come. It seemed outrageous to me that an arms race was allowed to happen. The newspaper was so full of doomsday scenarios that it made me feel it was inevitable that the world would be destroyed by some nuclear accident. There was no guarantee the world would last long enough for me to grow up, have children, and lead a full life. I lived with a low-level but constant sense of dread. I also began to resent the way people in the newspaper said, day after day, how villainous the Soviets were. I felt like I was being lied to, that Russians were being demonized. It was something I felt in the pit of my stomach, an underrated organ as a natural arbiter of truth. So when it came to the so-called "evil empire," my gut told me we were not getting the whole story. The Soviets were painted as the enemy, but I knew they couldn't be all bad. When I enrolled at Duke University, I chose a Russian language and literature course.

I arrived on campus in Durham, North Carolina, with a deep tan and wild, bleached-blond hair. I didn't look anything like most of the other girls, with their sweater sets and tennis bracelets. The place was swarming with Southern belles, and my bohemian look stood out, with my masses of curly hair, exotic features, and thrift-shop fashions. My first roommate was half-Indian and half-black, and the black students assumed I was some such combination as well. The black sororities rushed me along with my roommate. Originally I planned to be a philosophy major. My mother taught me that education was a goal in itself, not a means to an end. I knew that the more unmarketable my major, the more my mother would approve of the choice. She looked down her nose at people who were good at making money. "The merchant classes," she'd say with a sniff as she wrote out another likely-to-bounce tuition check to Duke.

I gravitated to the Slavic department. My Russian language professor, Bogdon Bogdanovich, was tall, lanky, and a bit disheveled. He was handsome in a dangerous kind of way, a man who looked as if he could make himself comfortable in the beds of many women. I fell instantly, madly in love with him and knew I had to be in the Russian department. Bogdon was a sign. He was married and he was my professor, making him off-limits. My attraction to the unavailable began. At the same time, I began my infatuation with Russia, the place of my father's origin. I wanted to know the enemy. I couldn't know my father; it would have been too much of a betrayal of my mother. So I took a circuitous route to find him, crossing the ocean, the world, and enemy lines, to Russia.

Love *à la Russe*

I met Dima in my quest for a decent meal. As a visiting university student in Russia in 1980, I was obsessed with finding food. I lived in a bleak, poorly heated dormitory on the outskirts of Moscow and found it hard to adjust to the challenge of day-to-day life in the Soviet Union. It was still five years before Gorbachev and perestroika appeared on the scene. The food was unbearable. The cafeteria served gray sausages for breakfast, lunch, and dinner. The surly cooks did not seem to care, but then they snarled at us when we returned our plates, meals uneaten. Out on the streets, in the drudgery so well known to the average Soviet, workingmen's eateries offered soup that tasted like dirty dishwater with a hunk of gristle and a rotten potato on the side. Some of the other American students appeased their hunger by befriending marines at the American embassy and getting invited there for specially imported hamburgers. Others of us, hungry for the true Russian experience, toughed it out. That meant wandering the streets of Moscow, ever searching for food. It brought me adventure, even when my stomach remained empty. I explored Moscow's extraordinary museums overflowing with cultural riches of its czarist past. I loved the parks full of monuments, gleaming statues of cosmonauts heading into space and muscled Soviet woman workers toiling toward a bright socialist future. I ventured into Russian bathhouses, where naked strangers engage in the peculiarly pleasant experience of pouring buckets of hot water over one another and beating one another with eucalyptus branches. "We are all equal in the bathhouses," Russians would say to me.

One day I got lucky. A fellow student took me to the home of a fashion designer named Slava who lived in an elite apartment in the center of Moscow, on Marx-Engels street. In contrast to the daily drudgery outside, there was a hidden, colorful world of privilege and comparative luxury. It was my first peek at the dual world that then existed in the Soviet Union. At Slava's there were always beautifully dressed people, and delicacies like French cognac and imported chocolate. Slava's was a bastion of comfort in an otherwise gloomy environment.

On one of my early visits, I noticed a young Russian man with enormous sad brown eyes. His name was Dima, and he was the most handsome Russian I'd ever seen. He was learning fashion photography in order to immortalize Slava's creations. He often entertained us with songs and jokes. I fell for Dima the moment he opened his mouth and started singing. I thought I had never heard a more sensual voice, and could listen to him for hours. It was as if he had just stepped out of one of the nineteenth-century Russian novels I had been studying. Dark and melancholic, he sang Cossack ballads and made fun of a regime that did not have much of a sense of humor. All the harshness and bleakness of Russia's soul reverberated warmly in his gravelly baritone. His favorite pastime was singing renditions of Vladimir Visotski, a banned Russian singer whom nobody was officially allowed to listen to but everyone secretly loved. On the anniversary of Visotski's death, Russians would congregate with bootleg recordings of his verses, which were reminiscent of Bob Dylan, and gave voice to the dreariness of average Soviet workers' lives. In parks, people would gather, singing the outlawed words, posting the lyrics to trees in tribute.

Dima introduced me to many underground cultural heroes, opening a spiritual world as rich and forbidden as the food at Slava's. The authorities proudly displayed Lenin's pickled body in Red Square, solemnly marching schoolchildren and tourists past his hallowed resting place, yet Dima showed me how ordinary people discreetly paid homage to their forbidden icons. He took me to the grave of Boris Pasternak, the banned Russian poet and author of *Doctor Zhivago,* where devotees would gather and recite his contraband verses aloud to one another. Dima also took me to a downtrodden Moscow alley where literary pilgrims made the journey to another shrine, the onetime home of Mikhail Bulgakov, author of *The Master and Margarita,* a banned classic work about the devil turning up in Moscow and causing havoc, a thinly disguised allusion to Stalin. Bulgakov fans painted the hallways of the old apartment block with passages and figures from his book. The authorities constantly painted over the graffiti, but Bulgakov's admirers always returned to keep their hero alive the only way they could. I delighted in their subtle defiance. I loved this hidden world, and I fell in love with Dima.

The truth is, I loved Russia. I was hooked as soon as I stepped out onto the cobblestones of Red Square and caught my first glimpse of St. Basil's Cathedral, with its colorfully painted gingerbread cupolas, so magical it looked plucked out of a fairy tale. On the other side of the square was the solemn, somber, modern Soviet tomb encasing Lenin. It all clashed, yet coexisted. The lack of distractions of capitalism heightened the appreciation of whatever small unexpected pleasures life doled out. Some Cuban bananas on sale outside the metro stop or a plastic cigarette lighter from the West could make someone's day. In those days, Russia had a genuineness of spirit born of hardship and a sense of community. Russians would always share what little they had with one another. Moscow was cold and severe on the surface, but the dismal totalitarian sameness could not contain the warmth and earthiness of its complex soul. It was refreshing to someone brought up in New Jersey in the 1970s in a culture of shopping and consumerism. The Soviet Union was giant, unruly, chaotic, and constantly in conflict with itself. Nothing worked. It was full of tragedy. It repelled me and at the same time attracted me, just as my Russian-blooded father did.

Russia felt like one giant dysfunctional family. I was perfectly at home there. As in any dysfunctional family, one puts on a brave front no matter how bad it is inside. Russia, for many years, pretended that its armed forces were a real threat to the West when it couldn't even feed its soldiers. I could relate to this way of being tough on the outside and a fragile, quivering wreck within; I'd been operating like that for years. One day the chaos couldn't be hidden anymore and the Soviet Union fell apart. I would have my own unraveling as well.

I attended the Pushkin Institute in Moscow. Our dormitory in Moscow had been built for the judges for the 1980 Olympic Games, held in August just before our arrival. This building was supposedly better constructed than most others, designed to impress the Olympic judges who were coming from around the world. But the countries the Soviets most wanted to dazzle, with their fancy sports facilities, newly built swimming pools, and high-tech skating rinks, boycotted the games because of the war in Afghanistan.

The Soviets still employed the czarist Potemkin-village approach of creating a facade of well-being and bounty for visiting dignitaries, while hiding a far grimmer reality behind a wall. During the Olympics, the authorities kicked out all prostitutes and indigents and spruced up Moscow. Insulted that the United States didn't show up, they had to make do with showing off to a motley group of American language students. Before we had even unpacked our bags, we were dragged off to the Olympic village to admire this great achievement in Soviet sports venues. One of my first images of the country was that bleak, scruffy-looking empty stadium. They wanted us to admire it. "This is bigger than any stadiums you have in the United States," our tour guide announced with pride. I asked questions eagerly, despite my lack of interest in sports. I felt sorry for the Russians, and hoped that my enthusiastic interest would make them feel better.

The new building we were living in was supposed to impress us, but the walls of our dormitory were already crumbling. I shared a tiny room with two other American girls. The Vietnamese students, who lived down the hall, always looked cold and miserable, bundled up in parkas they never seemed to take off. Our dormitory was situated on the outskirts of Moscow, and we assumed that the authorities preferred to keep us contained. The harder the commute into central Moscow, the less we might stray into ordinary Soviets' lives. I was determined not to be caged and went into the city all the time.

One day I arrived at Slava's to find Dima alone, and badly upset. An acquaintance had told him that Slava was gay. It had been evident to me, from the way he doted on men and surrounded himself with attractive male models. I had assumed that everyone else who visited Slava's place knew too, but it was never discussed. At that time, although homosexuality officially didn't exist in the Soviet Union, it was cause for imprisonment. Most Russians had little awareness of it; they believed official propaganda that homosexuality was one of those decadent capitalist diseases that afflicted only the West. Dima was mortified to learn the truth about Slava, whom he considered an adopted father. To make matters worse, Dima discovered that many friends assumed he was living at Slava's as a lover, when in fact he was Slava's protégé. Dima's own parents had divorced when he was five and he didn't feel wanted by his mother or father. Both had remarried. Slava had a real son who showed little interest in his fashion world. Slava saw Dima's potential as a photographer and had taken him in, looked after him, cultivated his talent, and treated him with a love and respect Dima had never felt from his parents. Dima was so hungry for that kind of attention that he had never looked closely at the rest of Slava's life.

Now in a panic, Dima confided his fear in me, the outsider. It was too embarrassing, and too politically sensitive, to talk about with his Russian friends. It drew us closer, and our strange romance began. Dima's first impulse might have been that he needed me to save him from his shame about Slava. He might have considered my main asset to be my coveted blue passport. I could not see clearly. I had such a crush on him, I was ready to accept any connection I could make with him. It felt good to be so needed, and in my twenty-one-year-old wisdom, I calculated that Dima would be tied to me so tightly that he would never leave me. But it didn't really work. We spent one night together on his foldout bed. He seemed distracted, just going through the motions, and it made me feel unwanted. I often felt insecure next to all the beautiful Russian models and actresses Dima knew, dressed in their black-market fashions. I wore layers of clothes for warmth, and intentionally erred on the dowdy side, sensitive to the way that other Russians might feel bad if I had better things than they. As a result, I often felt like a poor relative.

A couple of weeks after Dima's revelation, he pulled me into the dingy corridor of the House of Fashion, where we had gone for a glitzy fashion show of Slava's latest designs, clothes that no Soviets could afford.

"I think we should get married," Dima blurted out in Russian.

I didn't understand at first. My Russian wasn't perfect, and it didn't feel like a real proposal. It was not the romantic setting I had always imagined for the moment of my engagement. But Dima was insistent, and his meaning became clear.

"It's the only way we will know if we can have anything together," he went on. "Otherwise you will leave and we won't ever know."

I don't know if I was more smitten by Dima or by Russia. There was also an element of guilt, and my sense of responsibility. I knew that once a Westerner entered a Soviet's life it was changed irrevocably, since the authorities saw Soviets who openly met with foreigners as tarnished goods, betrayers of the motherland. I felt a swirl of emotions. I said yes. It was an even swap. He would get America. I would get Russia.

Cold-war Bride

When Dima and I turned up at the dingy gray office where Soviet couples went to register for a wedding date, we were told there was a three-month waiting period. It was typical enough of Soviet bureaucracy, but we panicked. My student term was coming to an end in six weeks, and I would be forced to leave, since it was virtually impossible to extend a visa. Dima quickly came up with a plan. He did not want to let his ticket out of the country slip through his fingers so easily.

"If we tell them you are pregnant, they'll give us an earlier date," Dima said.

"Great idea, Dima. Only problem is, I'm not."

Russians are great improvisers. "No problem," Dima said. "I know somebody who is."

·   ·   ·

I made an appointment at the British embassy clinic to get a document proving I was pregnant. Dima met me on a street corner in the frigid winter air at the appointed time, and he handed me my fake urine sample, which was sloshing around in the bottom of a vodka bottle.

"Whose is it?" I asked. I was curious about the murky color, often a sign of venereal disease.

"No problem, she is a seven-months-pregnant hooker," Dima said, proud of his find. "It only cost me fifteen rubles."

No problem, I thought, unless the doctor discovers I have syphilis as well as enough vodka in my urine to supply a Russian battalion. I hoped the hooker had at least finished the vodka before peeing into the bottle. Dima wasn't allowed into the embassy grounds so I waited alone in the reception area. It gave me a moment to wonder why I was doing this. I was afraid if I didn't go through with it, I would lose him. But was that such a bad outcome? And what if the doctor realized it was a hoax?

The doctor did not notice anything amiss with my bootlegged urine, and we got the stamped document that the Soviets required. Nothing was ever done in the Soviet Union without an official-looking stamp and copies made in triplicate with messy carbon paper. In those days, Xerox machines were banned, seen by the authorities as a pernicious tool to disseminate underground information, or samizdat, as the Russians called contraband material printed at home. Yet the bureaucrat at the marriage registry, apparently seeing it as her task to defend Soviet males from Western corrupters, would not accept the document. No explanation. No exceptions. We had to wait the three months. Not even a pile of bribes, in the form of Ralph Lauren cologne, Belgian chocolates, and a Fendi scarf, persuaded her to relent.

Defeated, I went back to New Jersey. It was strange to be home. I had finished college and didn't know what to do with myself. I missed Russia. I found it hard to explain to any of my friends or family what it had been like there, living in a bizarre kind of poverty with all the romance of brooding Russia. It was so far away, so removed from the United States. I spent days lying on my mother's sofa watching TV shows. *General Hospital* and *The Dating Game,* it seemed, helped me reconnect with my country.

I eventually got a job in a restaurant, where I met Lori, who became my best friend. I was a waitress; she was the manager. Having trouble with authority, at first I didn't pay much attention to her, since she was technically my boss, but it soon became clear to me that she had earned her status because she had a certain innate wisdom beyond her years. She too was half-Jewish and half-Protestant. Lori was a fellow traveler and easily mingled in other cultures.

We quickly became close. She was fascinated with Russia and wanted to come see the place for herself. She listened sympathetically to my endless fretting about Dima. I could not decide what to do. I changed my mind a hundred times. One day I would be convinced I could not live without him, that I had to go back and save him. The next day I would think going back meant becoming entangled in a green-card marriage with a man who was not really in love with me. I felt stuck, neither option giving me any comfort or relief. After a couple of months and many counseling sessions from Lori, I came to my senses. "Men are complicated enough; why make it any harder by marrying someone from a different planet?" she said.

The day before my planned departure I got up the courage to call Moscow.

"Dima, I've decided not to come."

At first there was silence. Then came a reply made more haunting by the static of thousands of miles of cable under the Atlantic Ocean.

"But then I must put a gun to my head," he said.

I thought he was serious. I was not familiar yet with the melodramatic nature of Russians like Dima—who, I discovered later, often threatened suicide just to get his mother to do his ironing or to get a friend to pick up a restaurant tab.

I found myself on the next Finnair flight to Moscow via Helsinki, one of the few routes into the Soviet Union in those days, since direct flights between the United States and Moscow did not yet exist. A Finnish woman seated next to me asked why I was heading to Moscow. "I'm getting married," I told her. But I half felt as if I were lying.

Sometimes we sleepwalk through events in our lives, only to understand how they fit into our particular cosmic weave much later. Some people use alcohol or drugs to dull their pain. I used love. I sometimes wondered if I married Dima because he was the first Russian male I met who was sober enough to walk down the aisle.

It wasn't exactly an aisle. Dima and I were married at the Central Palace of Marriages in Moscow. A small, round, scowling woman, with a big pendant emblazoned with Lenin's likeness nestled in her heaving cleavage, performed the ceremony. I had to borrow a dress from another American student, as there was nothing in any store in Moscow that I would consider wearing. I did not make any of the normal bridelike preparations, nothing old, nothing blue, just a desperate attempt to get rid of my hangover. I woke up that morning with swollen eyes from a night of drinking. The floor lady, or *derzhurnaya*, whose job it was to hand out keys so she could spy on the Cosmos Hotel's guests, gave me tea bags to put under my eyes, promising that the tannin would bring down the swelling. Russians are masters at fixing all maladies brought on by alcohol, and have endless sympathy for hangovers. The same floor lady who fussed over me that day would have happily ratted on me for having a Soviet citizen in my room, since they weren't allowed in hotels for foreigners. To get inside, they had to endure the humiliation of standing outside in the cold to get a *propysk,* or pass, though entering their name on a list—sure to be turned over to the KGB—was something few Russians wanted to do.

Dima's adopted father, Slava, turned up at the appointed time on that snowy March morning, bringing a few of his friends. One of the American girls I knew who was still studying in Moscow came. Otherwise I had nobody there of my own. Just before we went into the large red hall for the ceremony, we were offered music for an additional four rubles. For twelve rubles, we could get the event recorded on eight-millimeter film. I splurged on both. I wanted to do the traditional thing Soviet couples do and place flowers on Lenin's tomb after the ceremony. Dima would not have it. At our hastily thrown-together wedding party afterward, we ate tinned peas and gelatinized fish and drank lots of vodka. There was no cake. The ten or so guests beat their fists on the table as they chanted, *"Gorky!"* which means "bitter," perhaps an apt emotion to evoke at the start of a marriage, given the high divorce rate among Soviets. It is a tradition that signals the newlyweds to kiss. Dima was reluctant, continuing instead to tell a joke to an elegant redhead seated on his other side. I had to hold back my tears: I felt so alone. It was not how I had pictured my wedding day. I barely knew him. He did not seem to love me, yet he vaguely reminded me of my father. When I asked myself why I was there, I just felt blank and stuck. I knew I was being stupid and destructive, but I felt compelled to carry on. The vodka helped.

Now I had a handsome foreign husband who could not leave Moscow. Despite the marriage, the authorities wouldn't give him exit papers. The obstacle was that his mother worked in a military installation, and that theoretically put Dima too close to state secrets that might be passed to me. It was a minor detail that Dima had overlooked in his scheme to get out of Russia. But he would not give up hope. Every six months he would apply to leave the country. He was refused again and again. It left him in a kind of legal limbo. The mere act of applying to leave the Soviet Union made him persona non grata with the authorities. He could not get a job officially, and was pegged as a target of suspicion. Many of his friends wanted nothing to do with him, worried that his stigma as a refusenik would rub off on them.

Yet each time Dima got a refusal, I was secretly relieved. Once he got his exit permit, I would lose Russia. At the time, foreign spouses were granted visas for only three months, so I would visit for short periods of time. Despite the hardships of living there, I was completely hooked on Moscow. Our relationship, imperfect as it was, gave me an incredible opportunity to live life from the perspective of a Soviet citizen, deprivations and all.

As a student I had relied on the dorm cafeteria in order not to starve. Now, on my own, eating and shopping were the first survival skills I had to master. They were difficult tasks in a country where food shops tended to be empty or left with a paltry selection of unappetizing choices. There was usually little more than tins with something resembling cat food, or rancid tomato sauce, or slabs of coagulated grease and gristle with a speck of meat, known as *kolbasi*. The shops did not bother trying to entice customers with catchy names. The milk store was called Milk, the meat store, Meat, the vegetable store, Vegetables. In fact, those names were themselves deceptive, since there was rarely anything in the vegetable store that was even remotely green, just a few sprouting potatoes and a rotting carrot or two. The milk store never seemed to have any milk, either, just a lump of rubber that was passed off as cheese. I could never remember to bring my own bag. Packaging was a luxury Soviets did not bother with, and forgetting to bring your own invariably provoked the wrath of the beefy saleswomen, who were quick to berate me. The few eggs and potatoes I could find in a store would usually end up stuffed in my pockets.

I used to tell Dima we should start a diet clinic in Moscow, a cinch since there was not one appetizing thing to eat in the entire country. "Think of the fortune we'd make," I told him. "'Come to Moscow, guaranteed to lose ten pounds in a week.'" Russians just didn't understand how to market their country properly, I thought. But my husband was not amused. He could not imagine the idea of a place where marketing is designed to tempt consumers into buying because there is so much choice available. He was sure I was exaggerating about the bounty of supermarkets back home. He got frustrated with my descriptions of life in the United States.

"Sometimes I think you are a KGB plant and you make up all these stories of this luxurious life in the West as one more way to torment us," he said to me once. "The West probably doesn't even exist. They just train you at some camp outside of Moscow." It was hard to tell if he was joking.

When I did muster up the stomach to hit the shops, there was the fear of being trampled by the babushkas, who were perhaps the best secret weapon in Russia. Their average height was about five feet, three inches—so was their width, and they had physical power and aggression a hundred times their body size. They would charge off to the shops early in the morning, a stampeding herd of woolly coats and furry hats. Bundled up in multiple layers of clothing, they were insulated from the cold and also from each other. In Moscow's dilapidated public-transport system, they were constantly sardined into subway cars or trams. Their bulky attire might afford them a few inches of breathing room. Moscow's sidewalks were packed with people swarming to and from the metro. In contrast, its wide avenues were deserted. Few people had private cars, so the roads were traffic-free.

As many as two million people would pour into Moscow from the outskirts each day to try to buy milk or butter, which were unavailable a mere fifty miles outside the capital. Those lucky enough to have permits to live in Moscow also seemed to spend their days scouring the shops for food. A permit to live in Moscow was so desirable, it was commonly the basis of a marriage. Living space was in such deficit that couples sometimes shared their tiny apartments even after divorce. Many Soviets were still living in *communalkas,* or communal apartments, where several families shared a kitchen and bathroom.

A divorced policeman once told me he had to share one room in a *communalka* with his ex-wife. They divided the tiny room with a blanket not thick enough to smother the noises of his ex-wife's love-making with her new boyfriend. Life in the *communalka* was a prime source of satire for Soviet playwrights and filmmakers. For the average citizen, it was a glaring example of the indignity of the system. Privacy is such an alien concept, there is not even a word for it in the Russian language. When Dima and I registered for our marriage, we were handed a shabbily printed pamphlet telling us what to expect on our wedding night. Privacy is so elusive that the first piece of advice on the brochure was to be alone with each other— no easy task for the average Soviet couple.

Dima and I lived in several different places in Moscow. They all run together in my head, because they were almost all the same. The entranceways stank of urine. They had one room with a sofa that turned into a bed at night and a television set. Dima was addicted to old Soviet war movies, which was about all that ever seemed to be on. The kitchen was tiny with a small linoleum table with plastic chairs. The furniture was always the same because all the shops sold one standard-issue. Most apartments looked alike, with one style fitting all. There was one design for sofa beds made all over the Soviet Union, one design for chairs, one design for curtains, and one design for plates. Everyone had the same coffee table. To break the monotony, some Soviets would stick on the wall anything Western they could find, an out-of-date calendar or a poster advertising Pepsi. The bathrooms were divided: there would be a tiny closet-sized toilet, often without a seat, and ripped-up pieces of *Pravda* instead of toilet paper; next door there was a plain washbasin and a cracked, stained bathtub.

Sometimes it was so cold outside I went stir-crazy, unable to leave the apartment all day. Russian friends were always trying to introduce me to winter virtues such as ice-skating and walks in the snow. They found it invigorating, but I didn't. My feet and nose were always frozen and took hours to defrost after each foray outdoors.

Nobody in Moscow ever seemed to be at work. The streets were full of people devoted to scavenging the shops for supplies. Often one office worker would hit the streets and bring back booty to his or her coworkers. Shopping had to be a full-time preoccupation involving cunning, perseverance, and community spirit or Soviets would have starved.

I had no willing babushka or officemates as a network of people to pick up whatever they stumbled across during the day. I learned to shop without preconceived notions. I'd go as a blank slate and not expect to find eggs, butter, or milk—just be pleasantly surprised by whatever vaguely edible foodstuff I did stumble upon. I got used to Soviet life, to the wretched bathrooms and to the cold, to the secrecy and the fear. But I never could get past the food situation. I was always hungry.

Yet the friendship, generosity, and depth I found among Russians made up for everything the country lacked in creature comforts. When your mind is hardened by deprivation, undistracted by the temptations of a consumer society, you can spend more time with loftier thoughts. Russians shrugged off the daily hardships of life. Instead they would set the table with whatever they had, and drink vodka, recite poetry to each other, and sing late into the night. To me, they looked like gentle spirits trapped in gruff exteriors. Russia was like a narcotic for me, a place where suffering was revered as a high art form. Russians seemed to have cornered the market in tormented souls. My mother had taught me to worry about everyone else's problems and not dwell on my own, always reminding me that someone else had it worse. "Think of the soldiers in the trenches," she always said. I took her advice to heart. Here was a whole country that had it worse. There was no room for worry about my own wounds.

The simplest things in Russia often seemed intense, such an emotional roller coaster. Every friendship with a foreigner was fraught with danger, yet Russians were hungry for contact with the West. Many would take great risks to know me and learn from me about the world outside. I was their conduit to Western music, books, and a forbidden way of life. Many were desperate to know the lyrics of songs by the Beatles, or glance through a fashion magazine for a peek at Western life.

I would often meet Russian friends at a busy metro stop to keep from being noticed, and then we'd wander the chilly streets or drink knee-numbing port wine in the parks. We would discuss Solzhenitsyn and other banned works that I had read and they had not. I would often call them from a phone-box and never from my home phone, since I assumed it must be bugged. Outsiders like me could relay information contrary to the daily dose of disinformation fed by the government.

Even though I was married and living with Dima, few Soviets would risk having me in their homes. Those who did often had treasures to show me. Artists with a lifetime's worth of work hidden away in a closet or under a bed because it was not politically acceptable would sometimes make me the first audience to whom they could show their work, since showing another Soviet was a risk. The system bred distrust. Everyone was so worried about being bugged that it meant the KGB had less bugging to do.

Dima and I had a tumultuous time. It turned out there was another woman, a pretty blond harpist called Natasha. Dima was infatuated with her long before he met me. I gradually learned that she too was determined to get out of Russia and was shopping around for a Western husband. So she was never going to marry Dima. He insisted the relationship was over but I always wondered if they were secretly plotting to marry two suckers, use the marriages to get out of Russia, and then hook up together in the West. Sometimes he would go out at night and tell me I could not go with him. "It would be bad for them to have an American there," he would say. Naive as I was, I did not argue with that, worried that I might get someone in trouble just by turning up. So I never knew whether he was really going to see Natasha, or someone else. My suspicions were aggravated by Dima's lack of interest in me when we got into bed most nights.

When people in the United States asked if I was married, I would say, "Sort of. I was a cold-war bride," not sure if my marriage was a product of politics, or a victim of it.

My marriage felt like a sham. But that was the model that was familiar to me; that was what my parents' marriage had felt like. It felt uncomfortable, but it was a discomfort to which I was accustomed.

Over the years I would come back to Russia in various incarnations. I worked as a tour guide, bringing American doctors and lawyers on educational exchanges. I worked for U.S. television and magazine bureaus as a translator and interpreter of Soviet life, especially valuable because I straddled two worlds by living among the Russians. They were lonely years. I didn't feel as if I lived in one place or the other. My friend Lori came to Russia and met Dima and my Russian friends. Her knowledge of that part of my life bound us forever. She was the only one of my American friends who understood Russia's lure for me. For a while it infected her too, and she visited several times. As for Dima, since the Soviets were stingy with visas, I had to find all kinds of ways to keep returning to see him. He may not have been much of a real husband to me, but he was an extraordinary guide into the Soviet psyche, which looked so impenetrable from the outside.

4

An American in Moscow

I got my start in television in part because I was such a lousy housekeeper, a failing I inherited from my mother. Back in America and in between visas, I cleaned houses to earn money to pay for graduate school at Columbia University in New York. One employer, who worked at NBC News, was so eager to get me out of her bathrooms, she offered me a job as her assistant at NBC News in New York covering the elections in 1982. It was menial work, but once I got back to Moscow it opened doors for me.

I started working in Moscow's NBC bureau whenever I came back to see Dima, staying a few months each time. Because I spoke Russian, I could go out on the street with the camera crews and try to interview ordinary Soviets. Most of them were too afraid to talk to us, but a few would. Sometimes we would stand in the cold in Pushkin Square asking person after person to answer a simple question about their lives, but they would move past us hurriedly, hoping nobody noticed the brief contact they had with the foreign media.

My job also opened a new realm of conflict with Dima. He was always trying to get me to help myself to supplies from the NBC office. There were cupboards full of imported cleaning fluids, paper towels, canned foods, peanut butter, and coffee. He could not understand why I was so reluctant to take whatever wasn't locked up. Any self-respecting Soviet worker would consider it a duty to rip off his place of employment for whatever he could find, even though they would give the shirt off their back or their last ruble to a comrade. When everything is owned by the state, no one takes responsibility for anything. It was hard to explain to Dima why I was unwilling to steal from my Western employer. In Russia, it was expected. I did end up "borrowing" an occasional roll of soft, American toilet paper from the office, but Dima was always disappointed in me.

In the early 1980s, journalists and diplomats still lived in walled-off compounds shielded from real Soviet life. Foreigners shopped at comparatively well stocked food shops, whose windows were hidden behind thick black curtains so as not to invite the envy of ordinary Russians, who were not allowed in. These stores were benignly called *beriozkas,* or "little white birch tree," and foreign currency was required. Russian rubles weren't good enough for the delicacies sold there. Among the treats were Hungarian chickens and Finnish biscuits, genuine gourmet items in the Soviet Union, where no chicken in a store was ever edible. Occasionally I would slink off to one of the "special" shops with my stash of dollars because I could not resist a luxury like a bag of peanuts or a decent chocolate bar. I would invariably get caught by a curious babushka on the metro. Dazzled by the fancy packaging, she would interrogate me as to where I found such goodies, usually resulting in an embarrassed exchange when she realized I was privileged enough to shop where she could not. I hated those moments. I wanted her to know that the borscht she lovingly made for her family was much better than whatever packaged junk food I had succumbed to. Dima discouraged such weakness: he didn't like to see hard currency, which was like gold, wasted on mere food. He could put anything in his stomach and assumed I should too. Dima preferred we spent what few dollars we had on much more essential items, like his wardrobe.

As Dima could not get to the West, I was expected to bring the West to him. He easily tapped into my guilt about my good fortune to have been born in the land of plenty. Many Soviets did. It was sometimes hard to find the dividing line between opportunism and reliance on friends to do favors. Within minutes of meeting a Westerner, Soviets would size you up for your willingness to transport goods across forbidden borders. Everybody always wanted something—for you to sneak out a manuscript full of venom about the Soviet state or letters to relatives in Israel, or bring back a pair of Jordache jeans or a ski jacket or whatever. I often agreed because I felt I was so lucky to have been born in the West, thinking that the least I could do was risk being sent to the gulag to help veritable strangers. It made crossing any border terrifying, because I was always carrying something I should not have. To this day I get nervous on the customs line, even when I'm not carrying contraband. Russians never offered to pay me for any of the things I was asked to bring. They seemed to assume that all Westerners were loaded with cash and had bottomless suitcases. People with so little often have a huge sense of entitlement when faced with the sudden possibility of so much. But it was not all one-sided: in exchange, I would get a friend for life.

In those days, Russia was essentially a barter society. If a shipment of umbrellas came in, shopkeepers would squirrel away most of them to sell to their friends, leaving nothing for the general public. If you worked in a food shop, anything edible that showed up was hidden from ordinary shoppers and saved for your friends. A dentist would hoard the limited anesthetic for his acquaintances, charging a hefty fee and leaving those not in the know to rely on a few shots of vodka before having a tooth pulled. I once traded three pairs of high heels, a down jacket, and a pair of blue jeans to get a drunk workman to come and retile our bathroom and replace the cracked wooden toilet seat that splintered my bottom. When I was asked for a favor, I usually had trouble saying no, even if I risked trouble. People would ask me to bring them the strangest things, from prosthetic body parts to dog-grooming products to birth-control pills. Western condoms were a favorite item, since Soviet ones, called *galoshes,* tended to have holes. I brought telephone answering machines, bras, books, music, anything with Western print on it. In most Soviet homes there was usually a shrine to Western capitalism somewhere to be found, usually a faded Western container such as a plastic Coke cup, washed and rewashed until the print had come off of it, or an airline calendar poster. Cheap packaging, which a Westerner wouldn't think twice about tossing out, was treasured by Soviets, symbols of the forbidden. Soviets saved plastic bags from the West with ads in English printed on them. Marlboro was a favorite. English-language T-shirts were worn threadbare. Anything to transport them even for a moment from their usual world of shoddy goods. I would also bring suitcase loads of the latest fashion items or camera equipment to boost Dima's budding career as a fashion photographer in the most unfashionable capital in the world. My efforts weren't always appreciated.

"These aren't the right Timberlands," Dima said once, rejecting the shoes I had carried all the way from America. "I asked you for the ones with black stitching." My husband, the fashion guru, also memorized the styles he saw in the glossy magazines I lugged over.

No matter how much of a burden all the requests became, my sense of guilt for having more always prevailed. Especially when I looked at the lives of Soviet women. On one hand, the constitution granted women full equality earlier than their sisters in the West. Indeed, Soviets prided themselves on their courageous women pilots, glorious female truck drivers, and the first woman cosmonaut. But usually the women were burdened with two jobs, at work and at home. They were expected to pull their weight in the workforce, and were often given the most miserable jobs like shoveling snow or heavy lifting in factories, and they were expected to fulfill the traditional women's role in the home, shopping, cooking, and cleaning.

I once asked a Soviet woman what feminism meant to her. "The problem is we have no kitchen aids," she said. "We'd have no problem with the sexes if we had washing machines and dishwashers." Getting a man to help with the dishes was not an option. I had trained Dima to do them occasionally as a lark, but he would race out of the kitchen if a neighbor or friend came over, making sure never to be caught in the act. It would have been a stain on his manhood if anyone knew I had him doing women's work. The situation between the sexes often seemed archaic. After dinner I was usually left alone at the table talking with men while Soviet women went into the kitchen to clean up and talk among themselves. Communism brought a veneer of equality when it suited, but sexual roles seemed rooted in a medieval chauvinism.

Perhaps the worst indignities endured by Soviet women revolved around their sexuality. Contraception was scarce, and sex education was taboo. It was easier to get an abortion than a condom. The women I knew averaged six to eight abortions in a lifetime. Some had as many as thirty, sometimes resulting in sterility, infection, or death. Giving birth could also be brutal, dehumanized by a gruff, assembly-line approach. A few women delivered in the same room at the same time on cold metal tables with no anesthetic. Men were shut out. Gripped by an ancient superstition, society forbade men even to enter the birth houses. Most women held their newborns up to the window to show a husband who stood waiting outside, no matter how cold or how much snow was on the ground. Today in Russia there are a few progressive maternity wards that allow men inside, but for many it is still forbidden for men to be anywhere around the mysteries of childbirth.

Dima was an extremely talented photographer, funny and bright but petulant and needy. He was as incapable of love as I was in those days. I was in emotional limbo, tied to this man and this country. I often felt as though I were traipsing back and forth between two worlds at war with each other. I suppose I felt much as my father had, driving from his mother's home to ours, between the two enemy camps. My father's mother differed from my reserved Northern Irish mother about as much as a Muscovite from your average New Jersey resident. In some way, I too was following in my mother's footsteps by marrying young and moving to another country. I lost myself in an alien culture much as she must have by coming to America in the 1960s.

My marriage was not at all about suffering, even if that was Russia's favorite national pastime. Dima and I often had a good time. Laughing at Lenin was a favorite sport, and Brezhnev was a good target too. It was hard to know who was really running the country back in the early 1980s, but they would trot out a corpselike version of Brezhnev to wave stiffly on top of Lenin's mausoleum on state occasions. Dima did a great impersonation of that ritual. We spent a lot of time in a vodka-induced haze, doing elaborate black-market deals. We would sell off items of my clothing for next week's grocery money, surreptitiously handing over a pair of Levi's in a back alley as if it were a pound of cocaine. A pack of Marlboros perched at the edge of our table for the waiter to slip into his pocket would cover the cost of dinner in one of Moscow's finest eating establishments, a meal survivable only if one washed it down with vast quantities of vodka. We lived in a constant survival mode.

Dima took me to all his special, secret places rarely accessible to foreign visitors. It was an insider's tour of the part of the Russian soul that the Soviets had not managed to squash. He introduced me to Novo Devichi Cemetery in the center of Moscow, a veritable Who's Who of deceased Soviet society. Anybody who was anybody, but did not rate highly enough in the hierarchy to be buried in the Kremlin wall, is buried in this cemetery. Famous writers like Chekhov, Gógol, and Mayakovski were also moved in to enhance the stature of the place. There is a proliferation of headstones bearing the date of 1937, a big year for Stalin's purges. Resting nearby are Stalin's henchmen, responsible for carrying out those purges. My friend Lev, now a psychiatrist in Los Angeles, loved to show me around the gravestones. It makes sense that he, as a man who now makes his living penetrating human facades, had loved one of the only sanctuaries for historical truth in Moscow. Soviet leaders had been inventing and rewriting history for decades. They ripped people out of history books. Stalin removed all his enemies from the textbooks, Khrushchev wrote out Stalin, then Brezhnev did the same to Khrushchev. But in the cemetery, the past could not be buried. People who officially no longer existed in the history books could still be found here. Perhaps that is why it was off-limits to the general public until Gorbachev came to power. Dima had a well-known partisan grandfather buried there, so he had special clearance to visit the cemetery. It was one of my favorite spots in Moscow. Having done away with the afterlife, the Soviets were generous in glorifying the mortal world. Giant granite statues depicting the socialist contribution of the deceased stood in place of a religious symbol or plain gravestone. Famous cosmonauts were memorialized by towering spaceships. A famous communications expert was etched in stone with a phone to his ear. A well-known obstetrician was constructed with a baby in his arms. Some of the statues are so garish, I sometimes wondered if the immortalized were writhing in embarrassment below ground.

Another of my favorite haunts was the beer bars. They were usually down some filthy stairway, stank of urine, and attracted the low end of Russian society. I would go in and hunt down a dirty glass beer mug, take it over to the communal sink, and wash it out before placing it under a beer-dispensing machine. Then I would pop in my twenty kopeks and the beer machine would spit out some foul-tasting warm liquid that Russians called beer, with which they would wash down some salty dried fish innards as they stood slumped over sticky counters, standing in puddles of the spilled so-called beer. Had George Orwell visited this joint before writing *1984*? Despite the decidedly grubby surroundings, I loved them because I was always amazed at the level of conversation at those places. I would often end up discussing Tolstoy or Lermontov with some drunken bus driver.

I was also fascinated by the gas-water machines, a variation on the beer dispenser. In order to quench the thirst of the masses, the great Soviet state erected drinking machines on the streets in place of cafés or kiosks. One filthy chipped glass would be attached to this contraption. First you would turn the glass upside down and rinse it out with a few splashes of water to wash away the germs. You would insert your three kopecks and some yellowish colored gas-water would spurt out. It must have been an acquired taste that, despite my numerous attempts, I never developed. It made me think sometimes that the Russians must be a super-race, given the things they could consume and still survive.

As long as I did not delve below the surface of our relationship, it was exhilarating. Dima could make me laugh and laugh, when he was in the mood to poke fun at his country. Absurdity was in constant supply. Once I came across a line of people waiting for nothing. It was inside GUM, the cavernous department store on Red Square. Dima explained that at the same time each day, an ice-cream vendor turned up. People were just staking their place in line. I dubbed them lines of anticipation. Laughter was often the best defense in coping with the inanity and degradation of daily Soviet life.

Even with his irreverence for the Soviet state, Dima was sometimes touchy about me mocking it. One line he could not let me cross was Pavlik Morozev. I could make fun of Grandfather Lenin, as schoolchildren were taught to refer to him, but criticism of the little-boy hero, revered by Soviets, disturbed Dima. Pavlik was a Stalin-era invention. During Stalin's forced collectivization of the Russian peasantry, millions starved. Pavlik is revered for having turned in his kulak parents to the authorities because they hoarded a small amount of grain to feed *him*. The parents were executed. The son was lionized. Throughout the Soviet Union, schools and streets were named for him, statues were erected to honor him— the boy who betrayed his own parents for wanting to feed him. I did not understand Dima's attachment to this scoundrel. It was a sign of our cultural incompatibility. Maybe the esteem in which Pavlik was held was a good barometer for the health of the Communist Party. I knew the Soviet state was unraveling when I saw a small newspaper article in *Literaturnaya Gazetta,* soon after Gorbachev came to power, questioning Pavlik's stature. Things were changing, even though Pavlik represented a mind-set that did not die out with the Soviets. In today's democratic Russia, officials desperate to collect taxes resurrected that Stalin-era technique, urging children at one point to report their parents to the police for not paying their taxes.

Being a foreigner at a time when they were few and far between meant an automatic entrée into Moscow society. In the elite, artistic circles, it was fashionable for young Soviets to flirt with danger and have foreign friends, so I was kind of glamorous, simply by virtue of my passport. I had never felt like that before. My frizzy hair and lack of mainstream thinking always rendered me uncool when I was growing up in New Jersey. In grade school, I worried about sitting alone on the gym floor because I might be the last girl picked for the team. I dreaded lunch hour and the possibility nobody would want to sit with me in the cafeteria. Now I was hobnobbing with Bolshoi ballerinas, artists, and film stars who lived a privileged life in this so-called classless society. I often hung out at the Dom Kino House of Film, a private club for Moscow's luminaries in the movie world, where Soviet actors and actresses could dine on special stocks of food unavailable to the masses. They would carefully inspect one another's clothing labels, and were all glamorously decked out in the latest black-market fashions from the West. Ultimately just about anything was available in Moscow to anyone with money and the right connections.

To keep me humble, Dima and I always went home to our squalid apartment block, which resembled a barracks in the outskirts of town. We lived in one of those dreary five-story Brezhnev-era apartment buildings that all looked the same. A filmmaker even made a movie about a Moscow man who got drunk and ended up in Leningrad: after sobering up, he headed off to the same apartment block on the same street in Leningrad and never noticed that he was not at home in Moscow. In all Soviet cities, the streets were named the same, after Lenin, Marx, or some other socialist hero. The shabby buildings are identical, cut from the same design.

For a while we lived with Dima's grandmother in a two-room apartment, which tested the limits of whatever feelings Dima and I had for each other. Lybov Osipova was in her eighties and a true product of the Soviet state. A well-known doctor in her day, she had the distinction of being involved in Lenin's embalming, the pickling process the Soviets came up with to keep him from rotting while lying on display in Red Square for the last seventy years. It was offensive to this hero of the Soviet state to have a decadent American living under her roof.

"Dima, that capitalist wife of yours is showering every day so she can use up all the water," Lybov Osipova would say. "She's trying to weaken the Soviet state."

I would stumble into the kitchen in the morning, usually in a fragile state from excess drinking the evening before, to find her burning some gruel for her breakfast. I read Henry Miller to lighten my day. When Dima was home, we would laugh together. When he left me alone with my babushka-in-law, she would pretend I did not exist or did not understand anything. She would shuffle into our room, where the phone was, to call her cronies and complain about me as if I could not understand a word.

"She's always taking taxis, as if our metro, the finest in the world, isn't good enough for her," she whispered loudly into the receiver. Hanging around on the bench outside with the other disapproving grannies was her favorite pastime. She pretended she did not know me as I trudged back from the shops with whatever groceries I had managed to scrounge.

In the United States I entertained my friends with tales of good and evil from this distant world. In those days, Americans were fascinated by anyone who had been to Moscow, although their interest usually lasted only five minutes. After they were satisfied that their lives were indeed much better than those of their Soviet counterparts, their eyes would glaze over, especially when I would talk of the good things I discovered there. That did not fit easily into the picture.

Yet amid the bleakness in Russia, there was a lot of good. Russians without the distractions of shopping malls and the pressures of capitalist society had time for one another. Russian hospitality was boundless. No matter how surly Soviets looked on the street, inside their homes among trusted friends they poured out their hearts and souls to one another. Tongues always loosened with a little vodka. There was a stark dividing line between the inside and outside lives of Soviets: keeping quiet outside your trusted circle was a matter of survival; opening up to those inside your trusted circle, speaking soul to soul, as Russians like to say, was also essential for survival.

When I was there, I felt cut off from the world I left behind in America, I may have been in the heart of the evil empire, yet I had never felt so seen and understood anywhere in my life. Soviets were so anxious to know what the world outside was like that they listened intently to everything I said.

It was difficult to put a call through to the United States, so I was out of touch for months. My family were not big letter writers so I did not hear from them often. Then one day I got a letter from my younger sister, Francesca.

Dear Siobhan,

I have something really important to tell you, the most important thing I have ever had to say. XXXXXXXXXXXXX.
     XXXXXXXXXXXXXXXXXXXXXXXXXXXXXXXXXXXXXXXXXX XXXXXXXXXXXXXXXXXXXXXXXXXXXXXXXXXXXXXXXXXX XXXXXXXXXXXXX. I hope you understand.

Love, Francesca

The whole letter was blacked out as if censored. When we opened it on the metro I heard Dima's deep intake of breath. He was terrified the KGB had censored damaging comments from my naive sister. I immediately recognized Francesca's peculiar brand of humor.

I vacillated between loving and hating the Soviet Union. Living almost as an ordinary Soviet gave me a rare chance to glimpse life from inside another people's skin. But I felt like an impostor: not because I was an American living as a Soviet, but because I was living in a marriage that never felt real to me. Eventually I could not stand being in limbo anymore. I got sick of the snow. I felt like an alien in my own country when I realized I knew how to get around Moscow better than New York. I was more comfortable in the Soviet Union than in the United States.

Dima had been refused exit papers by the Soviets seven times. At each U.S./Soviet summit, the handful of unresolved divided-spouses' cases involving American citizens married to Russians came up along with the nuclear arms treaties.

By 1986, Gorbachev was in charge. While at my job at NBC, I

met Teddy Turner, who was working at another American news network, Cable News Network. He was the son of Ted Turner, who had founded the all-news channel just six years earlier. Teddy, who was working in Moscow as a sound technician, told me his father was planning to organize the Goodwill Games in Moscow. Ted, whom I got to know later, was disgusted with the way the Olympics and other international sports events had been constantly hijacked by politics instead of being used as a way to bridge political differences, so he decided to organize his own Olympics and exclude nobody. Instead he would hold them in the country that was often the one being barred: the Soviet Union. Allowing the Goodwill Games to take place at all was a sign that the Soviet Union was changing under Gorbachev's stewardship.

I liked the idea and was hired to help set up the games. It meant doing things that were unheard of in that country before Gorbachev had begun his process of glasnost, or openness. We arranged to bring in Xerox machines. It took weeks of negotiating and paperwork to allow such a dangerous capitalist tool into the country, but the Soviets finally relented. We arranged to have hundreds of frozen pizzas flown in, again with massive paperwork and permission slips to get them through customs. Ted Turner brought in hordes of people from Atlanta to put on this Western-style sports extravaganza. Many of them had never left the state of Georgia, let alone come to the heart of communism. In my mind, it marked a turning point. Gorbachev had allowed a trickle, but an avalanche would pour in over the coming years. For me personally, it was also a turning point. With the country opening up, I knew it was only a matter of time now before Dima would get his exit papers and leave Russia.

When a relationship with him was becoming a real possibility, and he was going to be able to live in the same country as me, I wanted out of it. The deficiencies in our marriage were magnified when Russia was no longer part of the bargain.

My work at the Goodwill Games won me a job offer in Atlanta with CNN. I decided to end my marriage to Dima, in spirit anyway.

"I'll stay married to you until you get out," I told Dima, once I had decided to take the CNN job. "But I need to take my life out of this holding pattern."

Dima and I were about to exchange each other's worlds. He was going to finally get his coveted America and I was going to get more Russia than I ever bargained for. Part of me was afraid to brave Russia without him. He had always been my guide. Now I would have a new ticket to Russia through CNN. But not before a detour to Atlanta.

Life on the Plantation

With everything I owned in the back of a used car, I drove south from New Jersey to start a new life in Atlanta. It was September 1986 and I was twenty-six. For the first time in my life, I had a real job with medical benefits and a pension plan. It was not exactly glamorous television work: I was going to be a tape logger. It was an entry-level job at CNN, a network that was still largely unknown, even in America. I was thrilled.

In 1986, CNN was still small, operating out of the site of an old Southern plantation, with a garden pockmarked by giant satellite dishes. The newsroom was in a basement, and at night the professional wrestling matches held on the main floor above us created a deafening thud every few seconds. Space was so scarce, with not nearly enough desks to go around, that many staff members were apportioned the edge of a desk. We had twenty-four hours of airtime to fill every day, and we had to do it with minimal resources, a small number of foreign bureaus, and a large number of inexperienced journalists. Such a fledgling operation felt like a family. I was at home in the quirky chaos and the constant crises. Just getting a simple story from a correspondent edited and properly broadcast on the air often seemed like a huge achievement. Many things could go wrong, and they often did.

I started at what might have been the worst job in the entire network, the overnight shift as a tape logger, labeling a huge pile of tapes. As soon as I had labeled some, more stacks were dumped on top, making me feel as though I were permanently trapped in the myth of Sisyphus. But it was what I wanted, a regular life and a regular job. Looking back, I realize that it was anything but normal, and that it didn't free me from my previously jumbled life. Instead, CNN provided me with a journey right into the heart of chaos.

The operation was run on such a shoestring that the pay was miserly. My salary was $9,000 a year. At times I had to sell the Soviet paraphernalia I had collected just to eat. A propaganda poster of Lenin might fetch as much as five dollars at a novelty shop in Little Five Points, the arty part of Atlanta. The lapel pins of Lenin as a youth went for a dollar each. Those often paid for my groceries. Atlanta seemed like a consumer's paradise to me after having lived in and out of the Soviet Union for almost six years. The supermarkets alone made my mouth water, they were so well stocked. I found that a trip to the bank or to the dry cleaners was a pleasant outing after the hulking heaviness of Russia. In Atlanta the sun shone most of the year; in Moscow I'd go months without a glimpse of its rays. Now I wore sandals instead of trudging through miles of snow, slush, and mud, my feet weighted down by fur-lined rubber boots in a futile attempt to fend off the cold.

One of the other great joys of being back in the United States was being able to talk every day to my best friend, Lori. After wan-

dering the world, including several visits to me in Russia, she settled down and married a man from the Italian island of Sardinia.
Even though they eventually moved to Texas, her life retained a foreign flavor, what with a constant flow of Sardinian relatives camping out at their home for months on end. They built three Italian
restaurants and are raising two children. I am the partially Jewish
godmother to her partially Jewish son. Lori was a stabilizing force
in my life, a wise witness to whatever was happening to me, giving
especially good counsel in the love department. She always helped
connect me to normal American life. She was the only person who
could get me to purge my closet of unwanted clothes, or finally rid
myself of unwanted men. I learned to accept her advice, always.

"What are we going to do with that husband of yours when he
gets here?" she asked, referring to my problems as ours, the way she
always did. I had been trying not to think about Dima and what
would happen when he got out of Russia.

Once I got used to life in America, I realized that I had not gotten Russia out of my system. I often felt nostalgic about the hard
days, foraging for food, living deeply with Russian friends, and
drinking vats of vodka. Sometimes I even missed the seedy apartments Dima and I had shared. I missed the mournful evenings
when his friends came over and we downed a bottle of cognac while
he played the guitar as we talked late into the night.

After almost seven years of rejection, in 1987, about a year after I
started working in Atlanta, Dima got his long-sought visa to the
United States. Though we had decided the marriage was over, when
he got out he had no place else to come but to me. We tried living
together for a while but it didn't work: he was so dependent on me
and I could barely handle myself in my new life. He had no trouble
becoming Westernized, but it made his interests change. Instead of
discussing art or philosophy or life, as we had so often in Russia, he

wanted to discuss ways to improve his credit, where I was little help, unable to get a credit card myself.

The first time he walked through a supermarket, he was in awe, amazed that an entire aisle could be devoted to dog food. Food was so plentiful, I pointed out to him, that they even sold diet dog food. As a consumer, he soon became picky and demanding, snapping at a less-than-efficient waitress or cursing when the market was out of his favorite brand of toothpaste. It made me wonder, Can the Russian soul survive only in tough soil? Does it wither when transplanted? After a few months, Dima moved out and went to stay with my mother in New Jersey to try to launch a photography career in New York. But despite surviving Moscow all those years, Dima found life in New Jersey to be rough and he couldn't stand my mother's dogs. Lori took him in. She had been prophetic when she called him "our" problem. He arrived just before Lori moved from New York to Texas. Dima took over her apartment and telephone, displaying a huge sense of entitlement typical of many Russians, acting as though everything that was Lori's, was his. Despite her patience, she had limits: she sent Dima back to Atlanta, where he moved into an apartment down the street from me. I helped him get photography jobs so that he could set up a life for himself in America. He took to it well. Being a talented photographer helped, but that was only part of it. Dima was a restless soul, the kind of person who was held back by the unreasonable restrictions on ordinary life in the Soviet Union and who flourished in the West. He has since had a great career as a photographer, and now travels in and out of Russia freely. Once he got a green card, allowing him to work in the USA, we divorced. Technically we had been married eight years, most of the time living on separate continents.

While working, I made friends with many of the unusual characters who turned up at CNN. Christiane Amanpour, who later became a star correspondent, was one of my first friends in Atlanta with a common background in Europe. We had both traveled extensively, and we commiserated over the provinciality of the place and our inability to find a decent croissant or bagel. Christiane was a secretary then, but she was ambitious, and willing to work hard for a chance at being a correspondent, giving up her vacation time to cover stories. Her determination eventually paid off.

My career at CNN was also blossoming. Because the company was young, it was easy to move up the ranks. Speaking Russian helped propel me from my lowly job logging tape to the International Assignment Desk, where overseas coverage was coordinated. I spent most of my time on the phone with reporters who were out chasing stories. We would work out how and when they would get their material sent by satellite or shipment to Atlanta from whatever far-flung location they were covering. I would listen to their adventures, marveling at how they had arrived at some ferry crash or student riot and filed a story within hours. I longed to trade places with them. I was again on the overnight shift, but I decided the best way to ever do what they did was to learn how to be a producer, so I started coming in during the daytime as well to train. Before long I had my first job as a producer, working on what was simultaneously the world's most boring and most fascinating news program. It was called *World Report,* a show in which few others at CNN were interested. But it was perfect for me.

A creation of CNN chairman Ted Turner, *World Report* invited broadcasters from countries all over the world to send reports to CNN each week, talking about their countries from their own perspectives. Instead of the usual CNN reporting, where a staff correspondent, often an American, drops into a country to become an instant "expert," these were stories from native reporters. It might sound like an obvious idea, but it was quite unusual. Most news organizations rely heavily on their journalists, who know how to prepare news for their audience, and CNN is no exception. The broadcasts that came into *World Report* were often unpolished and raw, and sometimes they simply represented the view of a government, since many news organizations in small or poor countries are state-run. Many of my colleagues at CNN felt that *World Report* was being used as a propaganda device for third-world countries. And some were certainly doing that. But no matter how heavy-handed the reporting was, it was an opportunity to hear a different perspective. Even if the reports were loaded with propaganda, there was often an interesting story within. And some were just plain funny. I thought *World Report* was visionary, one of CNN's greatest strengths. I enjoyed having access to unpopular views from pariah nations around the world, and I thought it an important symbol of CNN as a forward-thinking, global station. The job felt like a gift, tailor-made for my sensibilities.

For the years I worked on the show, I used to joke to friends that I was one of the best-informed people in the world. I knew more than anyone else about Zimbabwe's irrigation projects or Turkey's eczema-eating fish or Bahrain's famous hair-dancers. We aired everything without discrimination. Thailand's first contribution to the program was about a successful penis transplant. The Afghans would begin each report, "Dear Imperialist Viewers . . ." We took reports from places nobody else recognized as sovereign nations, like the Turkish Republic of Northern Cyprus.

At the time, the show was treated like an unwanted stepchild at CNN. Many of the network's bigwigs were embarrassed by it because the reports weren't flashy or well produced and featured bedraggled-looking reporters with strongly accented or broken English. It was not exactly a ratings draw. But it attracted a cult following of news-hounds looking for the exotic and bizarre, and information that was unsanitized by the normal Americanization of news. It was an opportunity to discover how other cultures saw themselves. When Iraq invaded Kuwait in 1990 and the United States, Britain, and other Western allies attacked Baghdad, it was a great outlet for opinions from the Middle East that ran contrary to those coming out of the State Department. But I had to fight to keep the show on the air during some of those weeks, since some producers didn't consider Jordanian or Iraqi TV's views appropriate. Like a protective mother, I argued that there was hardly a more appropriate time to hear the other side.

I also loved the motley crew of broadcasters from all over the world who used to traipse through Atlanta and visit us. I often found myself making dinner for a Vietnamese TV reporter or a Malaysian cameraman who was passing through, and that gave me a taste of international life in the heart of the American South.

At this point, I was still trying to figure out what to do with my Russian husband, and I ruled out other men from my life.

Except for the boss. Ted Turner was larger and louder than your average man. He is one of those people who fills up an enormous space with his presence because he is so alive. I saw him charge through the newsroom a few times and always wondered what he was like. One day he noticed me too as he passed by my cubicle. A few minutes later his secretary was on the line telling me Ted wanted to speak to me. "Have dinner with me," ordered a booming voice.

I was shocked by the call and afraid to go out with him. Dating the boss is dangerous in any company. But Ted, who is persuasive and determined, wouldn't take no for an answer. I agreed to lunch.

Ted was between marriages at the time, and he liked the fact that I worked on his favorite show. It turned out we had a lot in common. We both loved Russia. I admired the way he wanted to try to tell all sides of a story, even the most unpopular side. He might have made billions of dollars with his global vision, but his values were down home. He really thought he could help the world with his network. He wasn't interested in news that was merely titillating or sensational. I loved the way he believed that he helped bring about an end to the Cold War by improving communication between Russia and the United States through CNN and the Goodwill Games. And I loved the way he lived by his own rules. He decided the Ten Commandments were out of date, that people didn't like to be commanded to do anything, so he wrote up his own Ten Voluntary Initiatives and would spout them as an alternative at speaking engagements. Ted and I also shared a love of nature and wild animals. He taught me to fly-fish, to recognize the mournful wail of a sandhill crane, and to spot an elk herd on one of the vast expanses of land he bought to save space for the creatures who belonged there. He cares about the earth and its fate as much as anyone I've ever met. Ted would weep over an oil spill as if it had soiled his own backyard, suffer at word of a new war breaking out as if it were a rift in his own family. His shoulders seemed big enough to take on the world's pain. Mine weren't.

Ted was romantic and brilliant. But it was a full-time job being with him. And we were at different stages of life. Ted was fifty, already had five children, and was looking for a full-time companion. I was twenty-nine and had my career and children still ahead of me. "How about a baby white rhino to bring up instead?" Ted once said, when we were talking about children. "They're rare but I think I could get you one." I often felt like I needed a vacation after I took a vacation with Ted. It was like going to boot camp. Up at six to go fly-fishing, and a hike before lunch. Then he'd have a horseback ride planned or more fishing in the afternoon. Every minute was accounted for and he always wanted to stick to the regimen, hating changes to his schedule. And it wasn't exactly relaxing hiking or fishing, because following Ted's train of thought required more than average mental agility. Ted had a hundred ideas a day on how to make the world better. He took his wealth and influence seriously, knowing they gave him the opportunity to affect things. It was almost as if he were the only one strong enough to do it.

To me, though, it was exhausting to worry constantly about saving the world. I had plenty of my own problems. With him, I sometimes felt robbed of my own thoughts. It was such a relief when he fell asleep for a few minutes in his Gulfstream jet as we were flying from one ranch to another. I would be so happy just to sit and stare out the window or do a crossword, alone with my own thoughts. My brain may have been no match for his, but I did miss it. Ted wanted love and intimacy more than anything. But he wanted it so badly he couldn't seem to let it grow naturally with us. I sometimes felt he did not really know me and often tried to force me in a direction I did not want to go, like fishing. For my thirtieth birthday, I wanted to go to his place in Big Sur, California, to see the sea lions play off the Pacific Coast. Instead I found myself knee-deep in the Galatin River in Montana, having fly-fishing lessons. Lucky for me, the burly Montana native hired to teach me was getting a philosophy degree. We spent a lazy morning on the river discussing books and barely touching on flies.

Ted and I had a fight on that trip, walking in the mountains on his property, listening for elk and watching for bears. Ted wanted me to spend more time with him, but I felt a responsibility to my show, where I was a producer.

"I'll call your boss and fix it for you," Ted said. "Hell, I am your boss."

One phone call from Ted could destroy my credibility as a journalist, and I made him promise not to call anyone in that company about me. Of course, I liked knowing I could wield that kind of power, but I knew it would be better if I did not use it.

"How are we supposed to spend any time together?" he asked.

"Maybe we just can't," I told him.

But Ted hated the thought of anyone leaving him, be it a secretary or a girlfriend, and would not accept no. I was furious and stormed off into the dusky wilderness. After stumbling along for a while, fuming so intently that I did not look where I was going, I found myself alone on top of a mountain in the middle of nowhere. There was nobody around except, perhaps, a few brown bears. I felt helpless and scared and started shouting Ted's name. Standing up to him took a lot out of me, and I had pushed and fought hard to make a break with him, but now that I succeeded, I was petrified and lost. Ted's black Labrador, Sonny, found me about an hour later, a very long hour when I didn't know if I'd be found. Ted had been about to organize a helicopter search.

Our relief at finding each other patched over the rift for a while, but no matter how afraid I had been on that mountain, I knew I had to go my own way. However, the more he sensed my unavailability, the more he wooed me. He once sent his plane to bring me down from Atlanta to his Florida plantation. It was a grand old Southern mansion fit for Scarlett, and that night Ted fancied himself Rhett Butler. He opened the twelve-foot doors of the columned white mansion in a silk smoking jacket, with the theme from *Gone with the Wind* playing on the stereo. He even has a Rhett Butler mustache and a rougish quality.

After the fight on the mountain, we made a deal about my job: he was to keep out of my career, and I would stay with him. In a way, having Ted in my back pocket was like a nuclear deterrent. Everyone at CNN knew he was there, but I knew it was best if I never unleashed him. People who worked with me knew how hard

I worked, but I knew that others assumed I got ahead at the company because I was Ted's girlfriend. In the end, I concluded that Ted and I met at the wrong time in my life: my sense of self was still too fragile to get along with such a giant ego. But it was good for me to learn that money, power, and fame weren't what I was looking for in a mate. It was character-building for a girl who had grown up on food stamps to walk away from a billionaire. I felt I would never thrive or grow in the shadow of that enormous presence.

When I finally split with Ted, my mother was relieved. "He's unsuitable," she said on the phone to me. "I know a good mother would push you into this, but I just think you'll be miserable." My mother inherently distrusted anyone who made a lot of money, even if they were nice to animals. Ted has remained a friend. He and Jane Fonda, whom he later married, were both generous with me, often sharing their wisdom and experience.

Soon after Ted and I stopped seeing each other, I met a young intern named Alessio at the copy machine—from chairman to intern. Alessio had chiseled good looks, the light features of a northern Italian, and a gentle nature. He had come from Italy to spend a few months at CNN. I helped teach him how to produce a show. In exchange, he taught me to roller-skate. We spent lots of lazy days wandering around Atlanta's Piedmont Park and evenings cooking together. At first it didn't occur to me that I was falling in love with him; he was just barely a man. One weekend I invited him to go to the beach with me. When he sat down behind me on the sand and pulled me close to him I could feel how much I wanted him as a lover. But I felt like a jaded older woman and worried whether he'd even know what to do. A few hours later he dispelled my fears.

I was thirty; Alessio was twenty-one. I never expected our relationship to last more than a few weeks, and I think we stayed together much longer because I had no expectations of him. I never believed it would work out, so I never took the relationship seriously enough to get scared. Of the two of us, in many ways he was the older and wiser. He was far more domesticated than I. One of the first things he did after moving in with me was get us matching silverware. Alessio believed in living well. He loved to quote his father: "Americans don't eat; they feed themselves. They don't dress; they cover themselves." He taught me how to make a home. He brought me cappuccino in bed every morning. When he carried the TV and VCR into the bathroom during my bubble bath, I knew this was a man who understood me.

Life with Alessio in Atlanta had a dreamlike quality. It was the first time in my life that I felt truly happy. Alessio loved companionship, loved being in a couple. We had endless silly nicknames for each other and wore matching clothes. The days and nights rolled into each other as we snuggled, took baths together, and had comfortable sex. The only plans we ever made were for our next meal.

Alessio came from the sanest family I had ever encountered: it seemed modeled after some fifties-style happy-family situation comedy, but an Italian version. I had never met any adult who had a family he liked enough to vacation with. We skied each winter in Cortina, the exclusive resort in the Dolomites for the Italian jet set, to please his Venetian mother. In the summer we went to Sicily to his father's family castle. The usual rivalries between northern and southern Italians were played out between Alessio's parents, but it was playful banter compared with the cultural savagery that was waged in my home. Alessio had an idyllic upbringing with all the best schools and breeding. At twenty-one he spoke five languages. But no matter how loving and accepting his family was of me, I always felt defective around them. Yet I felt loved and cherished by this man who cooked and cared for me like nobody ever had. I had a real life with Alessio instead of some fantasy relationship with a husband living eight thousand miles away. And I could always disqualify him on account of his age, making sure he posed no threat to the walls protecting my inner sanctuary from real commitment. It was bliss. Until my career got in the way.

In August 1991, I was heading to Ireland for a family reunion of sorts with some of my mother's family. When I landed in Dublin, I saw a CNN report on a television in the airport, saying that hardline communists were trying to take over the leadership of the Soviet Union and had Mikhail Gorbachev under house arrest. I was stunned. I went directly to the Soviet embassy in Dublin and demanded a visa. With their country in confusion, the embassy staff was in a state of flux and doing some things out of the ordinary, like giving me a visa on the spot instead of the usual bureaucracy and delays. I called CNN and told them I had a visa in hand and was on my way. Then I called my mother to tell her I would try to make it for the second week of our vacation. I never got there; instead I ended up moving back to Moscow.

I hadn't been to Russia in almost five years, but it was only asleep, dormant inside me like a bear in hibernation, about to wake up and pull me back into its lair.

On the Aeroflot flight into Moscow's Sheremetyevo Airport, there was a giddy feeling among the passengers and even among the usually dour cabin crew. Everybody was drinking, not sullenly in their own seats as usual, but in a partylike atmosphere of excitement. Everyone shared whatever information they had about the momentous events unfolding. Even the captain spoke to us from the cockpit, updating us on the crowds out in the streets. I too was excited. I had a feeling the Soviet Union was in for some big changes.

The country I had known in the early 1980s survived on a system of badly concocted lies obvious to anyone who looked beneath the surface. The nightly news boasted of impressive harvests, yet there was no food in the shops. The factories were reported to be overfulfilling their production plans, yet there wasn't a pair of shoes to buy. They put men and women in space, but there was no toilet paper for sale. All governments distort the truth to some degree, but Soviet leaders seemed to set a new standard: every day there were blatant falsehoods about how great life was for the Soviet man and woman. "We pretend to work; they pretend to pay us," was a common saying in those days.

Now, in 1991, it was all coming apart. I never really believed the people had the energy to unmask the big lie. Actually, it seemed to crumble under its own rotting foundations. It was as if the country had a collective nervous breakdown, left with no choice but to overhaul everything it had once believed in. I was curious to see what lurked beneath. I had the sense that Russia and I were about to embark on a journey of discovery together, and I'd learn what lay beneath my surface as well.

The coup failed within days. For reporters, Russia was on the brink of a new and far more open society as the old ways unraveled. Newly reformed Soviet officials, anxious to behave like people in the rest of the world, started allowing us to go everywhere to film anything. The same stone-faced officials who for years had automatically said *nyet* to everything, now wanted to do things the way they thought they were done in the West, casting about for new rules to follow. Everything they had once believed, they were now told, was wrong. It was devastating to have to face the realization that their values, education, institutions, and way of life were built around a sham. They were like newborns in need of something to cling to. Naively and trustingly they looked to the West for all the answers. It took a few years before Russians realized the West wouldn't be showing them the way, and that they would need to search for it themselves.

A few weeks after the attempted August coup, the newly appointed KGB chief granted CNN permission to do a live broadcast from inside KGB headquarters. For decades Russians and Westerners had heard tales of the notorious Lubyanka prison underneath the building in central Moscow. During Stalin's era, political prisoners had been tortured to death there. A monument to the Polish revolutionary who had founded the secret police, Felix Dzerzhinsky, had dominated the square for years, as if watching over KGB headquarters. Just days before our broadcast, crowds had toppled the statue. People cheered while Iron Felix, as the giant statue was known, dangled from a noose as a crane removed it from outside the KGB building, which for so long had terrorized ordinary Russians. Here we were, laying cables through dusty corridors, flinging open windows that had been shut tight for years. The old KGB guards stood around in a mixture of disgust and amazement as representatives of the enemy they had fought for decades demanded more electrical outlets. When we asked to shoot a nuclear silo training center, it was no problem. Government ministers were now giving us their home numbers, all in their zeal to be open and normal.

Every day another previously hidden aspect of Soviet society was suddenly available to our cameras. The special Western-standard hospital, serving top party officials, let us in to film, as did the practically medieval hospitals catering to everyday citizens. We filmed psychiatric institutions, orphanages, atomic power stations. Before the breakup of the Soviet Union, we could get deported just for filming a bridge or other "highly sensitive" subject.

After I had spent two months covering the Soviet dis-Union, my bosses at CNN called one day and asked if Alessio and I would transfer to Moscow as field producers. It seemed like a dream come true, a foreign posting for a news organization that was emerging as a significant player in world affairs. My job would be to come up with stories to shape CNN's coverage, to travel throughout the country, to take care of the innumerable tasks behind reporting, shooting footage, and transmitting it for broadcast. I knew it was my chance to share the country I knew so well, which seemed so misunderstood in the U.S. media. I felt a sense of mission, to show the world that Russia may look big and threatening, but it was full of charm and delight. I also felt strongly that what happened in Russia was relevant and interesting to the rest of the world. The breakup of an empire was going to be a painful process, and Russians, often insecure and emotionally fragile, would need understanding from the outside world.

Alessio and I excitedly packed up our comfortable life in Atlanta and headed to Moscow. Once we got there, however, things were harder between us than I had expected. I distanced myself from him almost as soon as I landed, throwing myself into reporting on the chaos of Russia. Part of me was uncomfortable in the normal world he and I had created, and was relieved to be back in mayhem. I picked on him and discredited him in my mind, faulting him for not loving Russia the way I did. He kept his distance from Russians: perhaps not feeling as comfortable in the chaos, he preferred hanging out with other expatriates.

I quickly got swept up by life among Russian friends, old and new. Sasha Minkin, a theater critic who used to take me to underground theater when I was a student, was thriving under the new regime. In the Soviet days, the censors wouldn't clear plays of questionable content, so they would remain in terminal rehearsal, sometimes for years. Sasha had been daring, writing on the borderline of what was permitted by critiquing the system in the guise of theater critiques, rendering his work relatively unnoticed. Now, with glasnost, Sasha's criticism went far beyond the theater and he became a leading investigative reporter for the fledgling democratic press.

A woman I knew from my student days, a professor of Marxism and Leninism at Moscow State University, had become the editor of a glossy magazine teaching newly rich Russians how to spend their excess wealth on the finer, more decadent things in life. Some of my old friends, black marketeers trading blue jeans in the 1980s, were now becoming multimillionaires in the new Russia, starting up oil companies or otherwise exploiting Russia's vast natural resources.

In a desperate attempt to keep my relationship with Alessio going, I had the idea that a bloodhound puppy might help us, or at least distract us from the estrangement that was settling in between us. Anyone who has had any contact with bloodhounds knows that, of all breeds of dog, they are among the most challenging creatures to love. Nobody would go out and choose to have one except from ignorance or psychosis. Perhaps our psyches constantly re-create our childhood dynamics, either in the hope it will all turn out better the next time or because it is simply familiar. Just as children of alcoholics often marry drinkers, children of bloodhound owners go out and willfully get bloodhounds. My mother had grown up with them because her mother had bred them. We had had one, named Doucette, when I was a child. Doucette died tragically as a puppy, falling over a cliff, and I had always longed for another one. Just as a woman whose husband died young at war might idolize him, preserving forever that first blush of love, never having had a chance to get to know his bad habits, I too remembered only the cute floppy ears and sad eyes and none of Doucette's other more trying attributes.

Alessio and I went to the Bird Market one Saturday morning in search of a puppy to bind us together. The Bird Market is a strange place in the center of Moscow. Under communism it was one of the few places where free-market capitalism flourished and continues to do so in the new Russia. People come to sell animals of all types. Babushkas beckon buyers with conspiratorial looks, opening their heavy woolen coats to display kittens and puppies huddled against the cold in the warm inside pockets. It is a delightful place with birds chirping and exotic animals of all kinds, though the pain of Russia is also on display. I once saw an old woman crouched on the ice with her sad old red-eyed Saint Bernard named Charlie, the thick folds of fur on his neck draped with the medals of dog-show championships. The two looked as though they had been through a lot together. Nevertheless, judging from the condition of the woman, Charlie was about to be sold so she could buy another bottle of vodka.

There were no bloodhounds that day but we got word of where there was one for sale. We followed a lead to a typical Soviet apartment block, where a family of three shared their one-room apartment with three bloodhounds and a rooster, who was spitting seeds in a corner. Two dogs were lounging on the sofa and a third was curled up in a chair. I immediately fell in love with Sara. We took her home. She was big, slobbery, stubborn, and completely deranged. She also had a bladder problem that required a trip outside every two hours, even in the middle of subzero Russian nights. If anything, she contributed to Alessio's departure from my life.

"Siobhan, there are no bad dogs," said my mother when I called inquiring about some of Sara's problems, implying that any canine shortcoming is the fault of its human companion. Sara regularly devoured silk scarves and countless pairs of shoes, the newer and more expensive, the better. She especially loved to gnaw on Alessio's favorite antiques. Sara lumbered around dragging those long silky ears through the grime of Moscow's streets. She was oblivious to any command, lost in her own peculiar world of scents. She was a giant nose and ears on legs. Sara was such a generator of slobber that I was amazed anyone would come to my house more than once. She greeted visitors by shoving her wet jowl and snout into their crotch to get a good whiff. And then, after they thought they'd escaped her, she would hurl some slobber at them from across the room. Nobody left my apartment without being slimed. I thought I should start offering raincoats at the door. Every time I was angry with her, she stared at me with those sad, bloodshot eyes and my heart would melt. She was difficult to love, but I did. When Sara escaped in Gorky Park one afternoon, my world stood still.

"Don't let her off the leash," I shouted to Alessio as he headed out with Sara for an afternoon walk. Hours later Alessio returned to the office, ashen and alone. He had let her off the leash and, sensitive to any sound, she had bolted when a band struck up in the open-air theater in the center of the park. He had spent hours hunting for her before steeling himself to tell me. I was crushed. She was a pain in the ass most of the time, but the thought of the poor thing wandering around Moscow's busy streets alone and scared of every noise broke my heart. It was a good thing there was no news that day. I mobilized the entire bureau to recapture my runaway hound. Russians, usually the masters of sloth, can be transformed by a crisis: everyone, from the drivers and the cook to the workers renovating the office, stopped what they were doing to join the search. The cameramen took the TV lights out and roamed the park till three A.M. hunting for her. We put up flyers all over the park promising a ten thousand–ruble reward—equal to about a hundred dollars, and several months' wages in those days—for her safe return. We heard nothing encouraging, although I had calls all day and night from grannies who thought they had seen her, or just to offer their sympathy and support.

The staff in the CNN bureau put together a heart-wrenching video, pleading for Sara's safe return. Our bureau manager, Lena, was a world-class dog lover who regularly rounded up Moscow's strays and brought them into the office. We always had a number of homeless dogs living in the bureau, and I spent many hours calling around in search of homes among the expatriate community. One of our biggest problems with them occurred when we were broadcasting from the bureau: producers in Atlanta would ask what all the barking was about in the background. We usually lied and said it was packs of wild dogs in the courtyard below. We also made sure to clear out the kennel when the top brass came to visit. Lena, who I suspect may actually prefer that the CNN bureau forget news altogether and convert it to an animal rescue center, arranged to have the video shown on local television one evening. Meanwhile, I continued to ask everywhere about Sara. In the shops where customers were generally greeted with snarling indifference, the salesclerks stopped what they were doing to speculate with me about where she may have gone. Finally one old woman called to say she had overheard salesgirls in a confectionery store on October Square talking about a stray dog they had been feeding. That old Soviet habit of eavesdropping and relaying suspicious information that kept the nation in a state of fear for decades finally worked in my favor. My favorite driver, Volodya, a large burly guy who had jowls rivaling Sara's, rushed over there with me. We interrogated the staff, and learned that a stray bloodhound had turned up. A couple of guys across the way at the watch factory had taken her in.

We dashed across the street to the factory, where we put up more posters offering the reward. Word spread fast that a desperate foreigner was hunting for her dog, and two slovenly types turned up clutching what looked suspiciously like Sara's flea collar. In those days they didn't sell dog food in Russia, and certainly didn't have flea collars, so I knew they must have her. Dangling the collar in front of me as if it were a digit hacked from a hostage, they promised to deliver her once they were assured of the reward.

"I'll pay you anything," I said. "Just bring her back to me safely."

I'll pay you anything, just keep her, was what a part of me felt when they brought her. She immediately peed on the floor in her excitement at seeing me.

In a city of eight million people, word of mouth had been enough to find my dog. Soon after, my fear of her loss was replaced by frustration at her annoying presence. It was hard to keep her in a small Moscow apartment, and I even hired a full-time dog nanny for her. After a year and a half together, Sara and I parted ways. My older sister, Alexandra, came to the rescue the way she often did in emergencies.

Alexandra had grown up to live a quirky double life. She went from being a Peace Corps volunteer in the Philippines to the corporate world as a high-powered lawyer, albeit a slightly irreverent one. She climbed the ladder of success and became a supermom. She puts on Christmases fit for Martha Stewart, even if a slightly oddball one. She bakes homemade gingerbread houses and roast goose and trifle and then plunks down a menorah in the middle of a table laden with Christmas delicacies. She used her maternity leave to take her newborn son to Moscow in the dead of winter to fly MiGs with me. Learning of my dilemma with Sara, she managed to talk a family she knew in Athens, Georgia, into taking in a Russian-refugee bloodhound. When I flew with Sara to the States, it occurred to me that she was the second Russian I had aided out of that country. Sara later gave birth to eleven more of her kind, causing me some guilt for contributing to the bloodhound population of the world.

One of the reasons I had originally taken Sara on was gone: Alessio and I had lived under one roof for some time, but my heart had shut down. After a while, I pushed him so far away that he moved out.

Georgian Hospitality

By 1992 my personal life was in shambles, but my career was taking off. CNN prized breaking news—in a war zone above all. I got my first taste of war coverage with Christiane Amanpour, whom I had known in Atlanta, and who was already on her way to becoming a star correspondent for CNN.

At the time I was a rookie producer in the Moscow bureau, and Christiane had been sent in to help cover the collapse of the Soviet Union. We went to Almaty, a city in Central Asia where Boris Yeltsin and leaders of the newly unshackled republics were meeting to form a loose political union. About to fly back to Moscow, we learned that civil war had broken out in Georgia, the former Soviet republic, where the president had become so dictatorial that his rivals tried to overthrow him, reducing the capital, Tbilisi, to a war zone. Tom Johnson, CNN's president, was in Moscow to supervise coverage of the breakup of the Soviet Union. When we discovered that there were no direct flights to Tbilisi, Tom told us to charter a plane to get there.

I had never been sent to cover a war before, and was apprehensive, but as a new producer I wanted to hide my fear. It was my job to make all the arrangements to get us there and find a way to cover the story, and I didn't want to let on that I hadn't a clue what that would entail in a war zone. Christiane seemed confident and unfazed, as did Jane Evans, our camerawoman. Jane had lived through the worst of the fighting in Beirut, and Christiane had made her name in the Gulf War. I didn't want to let these two experienced war hands see how much of a chicken I really was.

We arrived late at night, and Tbilisi had completely shut down. There had been days of fighting in the center of the city. Zviad Gamsakhurdia, a poet turned president turned dictator, was holed up in the Parliament building. Opposing forces were dug in at a movie theater across the street. The once-fashionable Rustavelli Street looked like a shooting gallery. None of the taxi drivers at the airport wanted to go anywhere near downtown Tbilisi, so we were stranded until I tracked down an old friend, a Georgian doctor named Coco.

Georgians are among the most hospitable people in the world. They believe that a true Georgian must spare nothing to accommodate a guest, even if they are caught in the middle of a civil war. So without a second thought, Coco rounded up a van in the middle of the night and came and got us. He wanted to take us home and give us tea and food first, but we insisted that we had to get to the story, so he drove us into the thick of the fighting. We filmed the sounds of gunfire and burning buildings, and, with a couple of interviews, we filed a story within hours of arriving on the scene. Coco insisted on staying by our side at all times and introducing us to all the rebel commanders. He was horrified that we wouldn't stop to eat and was always trying to drag us home so his wife, Nina, could wine and dine us and he could show us off to his friends. We occasionally relented, knowing his wife had slaved all day preparing a feast for us.

Tbilisi is such a tiny place that everybody seems to know everybody else. They were all so friendly that I even wondered if they were actually shooting at one another, or simply aiming over one another's heads. As far as conflicts go, to a first-timer, this one seemed relatively benign. Nevertheless, rebel forces were shooting at Parliament, trying to oust the president, who had suddenly developed a totalitarian streak reminiscent of that other famous leader from Georgia, Joseph Stalin.

For days, Coco took us to see a ragtag group of rebels, sometimes led by a doctor from his hospital or some childhood friend. The Georgians had lived under the yoke of communism for so long that they weren't about to tolerate a new dictator now that the Soviet Union had dissolved. They are born entrepreneurs and have a deep independent streak. Nestled in the Caucasus Mountains, Georgia has a warm climate, and the verdant landscape contrasts sharply with the austerity of Russia. Many hills are covered by vineyards that produce famous wines, and Georgians boast that Winston Churchill's favorite wines were Georgian. Georgians are Mediterranean in nature and enjoy abundant and rich food, like shish kebab and spicy vegetable ragouts, unlike in Moscow. The Georgians we met were such devoted hosts that when we showed up, rebels would stop fighting in order to feed us. Whether it was a simple *hacha puri,* doughy bread with melted cheese and a fried egg in the middle served with wine, or a full-fledged eight-course feast, they could never let a guest go away with an empty stomach.

In the days that we covered the rebel perspective, all the renegade president's supporters were inside the Parliament under siege.

Christiane felt that we needed to get inside and speak to President Gamsakhurdia himself. It didn't seem like such a hot idea to me. Georgians may be gentler than your average combatants, but people were still getting shot. Just that morning Jane had come down to breakfast shaken up. A stray bullet had pierced her bedroom balcony in the night, missing her by inches, but breaking her window. She was undaunted, arguing that the rebels we were with would not fire on us if we crossed the square to reach the Parliament, while those holed up on the other side would know we were journalists. Perhaps the president's supporters would figure that nobody else in their right mind would attempt to run across the square dividing the two sides, even though plenty of people had come out to watch the fighting. As I would see in later wars, an incredible voyeurism draws people out to see the action, risking their lives. Crowds gathered on street corners to watch, at first tentatively, then inching closer for a better view. When the shooting moved too close and the bullets started ricocheting past their heads, they scattered. One day we came into rebel headquarters and found Coco's wife, Nina, there. She too wanted to see the action.

I was terrified at the thought of crossing the square, but as the producer and only Russian speaker, I couldn't let Jane and Christiane go alone. Coco tried to talk us out of it, but then, since we were his guests, insisted on coming too. It occurred to me how terrible it would be to have to explain to his widow and orphaned children that he had been killed because he was trying to be a good host to his crazy guests. But we were off.

Christiane went first, then Jane, then me. Coco came last. One by one we ran across the fifty yards of no-man's-land into the besieged Parliament. I was so terrified I couldn't even tell if anyone fired or not. I was breathless, immensely relieved to get to the other side alive. But my euphoria was short-lived, as it dawned on me that we'd have to run across the square again to get out of there. First, however, we had to try to get this madman to talk to us.

Gamsakhurdia's followers were surprised to see three women and Coco show up uninvited into their lair. Being Georgians, they could do nothing else but welcome us and offer whatever food they could scrape up. They rustled up some tea and grizzled salami sandwiches, eager to share what they had even though they were surrounded and had few provisions. It was Christmas day; the first of many I'd spend embroiled in a news story. I looked around this Parliament-cum-bunker at these mustached men armed to the teeth lounging about on sandbags. I loved Russia and always wanted to tell its story, but I had never expected this job to entail such personal risk. I wondered if I would ever get used to it.

We waited for hours, and finally Gamsakhurdia agreed to see us. He seemed deranged, with the crazed "I'll stop at nothing" look in his eyes often seen in guerrilla leaders or revolutionary zealots. As we shot our videotape, he rambled on and on. It almost didn't matter what he said: we had scored a major coup just getting an interview with him and being able to report his side of the story under such trying circumstances. In a blur, we ran back across the square to the rebel side of the street. We had been shipping our stories by air out to Moscow with fleeing Georgians, who were generally happy to carry a tape out for us for fifty dollars. When we got back to the hotel to edit our exclusive story, we learned the airport had just been shut down.

Our ever-resourceful Coco found someone willing to make the treacherous five-hour drive through the mountains to the airport in Sochi, the nearest city, to get our story out. Our producers in Atlanta were thrilled. However, we knew that although we had scooped the competition, it would take half a day for our tape to get out and on the air.

It was obvious that we should keep our scoop secret from competing television crews, especially after what we had been through that day. But humans, and especially journalists, often have a hard time keeping a secret. Sitting around the restaurant that night, the all-male NBC and CBS teams were discussing a possible plan to get inside the Parliament by stowing away in an ambulance the next day. They were desperate to get inside but were afraid, and probably rightly so, just to bolt across the square as we had. Jane, Christiane, and I sat in silence, dying to boast that the girls had already done that while the boys were sitting around debating the risks. Women covering war often feel they have to be braver and tougher than their male competitors, just to prove themselves. If we could wait a few hours, we could gloat to our hearts' content. But it was just too tempting to burst the balloon of macho bravado, and it slipped out of Jane's mouth. Jane was a female pioneer in the male-dominated world of cameramen and had taken endless amounts of grief over the years, so maybe she deserved her moment. The boys were shocked and hurried to match our story. That day other networks got to President Gamsakhurdia, but we still beat everyone else, getting the story on the air several hours before them, the kind of thing that reporters pride themselves on.

Many war zones later, I found out that covering a war is often all about that kind of bravado and, in some cases, an addiction to danger. Some correspondents give up their families and stable lives to push themselves to the limits of risk and endurance. Although CNN took care to provide flak jackets, lots of hardened journalists would never be caught dead in one, the wartime equivalent of seat belts. Staring death in the face and surviving can be empowering, and some people feel more alive by coming close to death. During that first trip to Georgia, I was such a novice I didn't even know that flak jackets were an option. I saw the soldiers in them, but didn't know we could have them too. Later, I was often embarrassed to bring up the issue of wearing one, because I didn't want to show how scared I was. We could always tell the new crew to the scene: they were the ones suited up in flak jackets and helmets. Camerapeople often resisted wearing them because they said flak jackets impeded their flexibility. That often made the rest of us feel like wimps for wearing them. As a result, we were inconsistent. Half the time we put them on after we found ourselves in the middle of a gun battle, crawling back to the car on our bellies to fish them out of the trunk. I saw people sensibly tape their blood type to the front of their flak jackets, but I never did the same. It made the reality of why we wore them too visceral. I became nonchalant about basic safety precautions—playing Russian roulette with my life. Like many other correspondents, I was deluded, thinking that danger somehow diminished each day I was there covering a war.

After I got back to Moscow from a few weeks in Georgia, I started working in my free time on my voice and camera presence. When I was out with a camera crew shooting a story, I practiced speaking in front of the camera until I became comfortable. On days off I wrote my own stories. It had become frustrating to do interviews and be out discovering all the quirky aspects of a story firsthand and then turn all I had found over to a reporter to write. Often that reporter didn't understand the language or hadn't been filming with me, so some of the nuance would be lost. I wanted to tell the stories myself. In a matter of months I moved up from producer to correspondent. That was one of the great things about CNN in those early days: anyone with the desire to advance could do so with a bit of perseverance and hard work and willingness to work through weekends and holidays. My other lucky break was that Eason Jordan was in charge. Eason never discriminated on the basis of gender. If a story breaks, he wants someone in there covering it, and never seems to care if the person is male or female. He is responsible for CNN having so many female camera operators and other women covering wars, unheard of at other networks.

My first big chance to report as an on-air correspondent came in autumn of 1992. The Moscow bureau chief was on vacation and I had been left in charge. Russian reforms were in a shambles and frustration was growing over the delays in reaching the prosperity that everyone expected after the collapse of communism. Russian politicians were looking for someone to blame. Boris Yeltsin, eager to protect his image as a popular hero, chose Gorbachev, his long-time rival. Yeltsin commandeered Gorbachev's newly founded think tank without telling the former president, who turned up to work one morning and found the doors of his office padlocked. The next day Yeltsin stripped him of his special government limousine and his dacha, or country home. That week I interviewed Gorbachev, who appeared genuinely hurt that after all he had done to avert violence in Russia, he was so unappreciated by his countrymen. Gorbachev had been pushed out by Yeltsin for his slow pace at reforming the Soviet Union and argued that a more gradual dismantling of the system would have resulted in less chaos. He warned that Yeltsin's decision to unshackle the Soviet republics would result in wide-spread bloodshed. With Gorbachev still popular in the West, I was on the air several times a day covering the spat between the two statesmen.

It was a great break for me. But I was also getting a lesson about how petty and childish politicians can be, letting personal animosities and political expedience override all other concerns. I was astounded by the intensity of the bitter personal rivalry between these two men. Initially they had been allies in the fight against old Soviet hard-liners, but in 1987 Gorbachev had insulted Yeltsin by sacking him as Moscow Communist Party boss. After Yeltsin took over the presidency in late 1991, he took every opportunity to pick on his former superior. He especially loved to take swipes at Gorbachev's relationship with his late wife, Raisa, expressing an old-fashioned Russian distaste for a wife's involvement in state affairs. Yeltsin often spoke with pride about how he kept his own wife out of politics. But he didn't always apply the same principle to his daughter, Tanya, who later played a significant role in his government.

I threw myself into work. And there was no shortage of news in Moscow to report, with one crisis emerging after another. One such story came when tanks in Moscow's streets began firing at the Russian White House, or Parliament, in October 1993. Yeltsin was locked in a power struggle with his old Soviet-style parliament, one of the last vestiges of Soviet power and full of disgruntled communists. They were trying to thwart his reforms, so at one point he dismissed them and called for new elections. It was democracy, *à la Russe*. When Yeltsin's vice president, Rutskoi, complained publicly that reforms weren't delivering all that they were supposed to, Yeltsin confiscated his government car and dacha, the favorite form of official torture. When Rutskoi joined forces with the parliament in an all-out mutiny, refusing to budge until their demands were met, Yeltsin shut off the White House's heat, then the electricity, and finally the water.

We had to cover the story in shifts, sleeping in the White House, waiting for the inevitable conclusion, knowing that an attack could come. We would prepare for our daylong turn inside as if on a camping trip. Given the amount of TV equipment we had to haul around, personal luxuries like sleeping bags and food supplies had to be minimized. As my camerawoman and I curled up on our coats, shivering one night on a bed made of two wooden chairs, we laughed at the notion that a few utilities being turned off would have any effect whatsoever on a Russian.

Yeltsin disappeared during the standoff, and I assumed he was out at his dacha, drinking. Outside the White House, crowds of demonstrators grew larger and larger as outcasts from all over the former Soviet Union made their way to the Parliament building. Nationalists and neo-Nazis, carrying heavy weapons, teamed up with genuinely democratic-leaning deputies who felt Yeltsin had no right to dissolve Parliament at whim. It was a bizarre scene, especially at night. We wandered around with flashlights, often turning a corner and bumping into a half-crazed zealot pointing a gun at our heads. In fact, they were quite harmless, usually just looking for someone to listen to all their frustrations. For many, the breakup of the Soviet Union not only robbed them of a subsistence living but of identity, so they banded together hoping to turn back the clock. In the news media, the story looked black-and-white—Yeltsin's democratic forces were beating back the evil communist resurgence—but as with most stories, the reality was gray. The lives of many decent people had been turned upside down, and they had legitimate gripes. Respected physicists, no longer able to survive on their salaries, were working as drivers for foreign news bureaus. We interviewed a doctor who moonlighted as a prostitute to make ends meet. For many people, the new freedom didn't compensate for the humiliation with which they lived in the new Russia.

Yeltsin eventually sorted out the standoff the way Russians know best—by bringing in the tanks. In broad daylight, they rolled down a grand thoroughfare called Kutuzovksy Prospect and, conveniently for us, right past the CNN bureau and our rooftop camera. As they started firing missiles at the White House, people out walking their dogs or with kids in strollers stopped to watch. In old Soviet fashion, regular programming was cut and the news was blocked from Russian TV stations. But in the age of satellite TV, those old Soviet tactics didn't work as they used to. Many viewers had access to CNN, where they watched as Yeltsin bombed his Parliament into submission. The news was presented as Yeltsin slaying the last gasping breath of communism. But it was hardly a democratic approach. All the excitement provided a needed diversion from my personal life. Alessio and I were still working in the same office, and it was hard to ignore the beautiful Russian nymphets who were always dropping by to see him. My suitors were limited. All I had had was a fan letter from a desperate farmer telling me there were no women like me in Idaho and that after seeing me reporting from inside the Russian White House, he had fallen in love. And, in Uncle Leon's increasingly frequent letters to me, was a warning of my impending spinsterhood.

Dear Siobhan,

I caught some of your recent reports on the television. I was thrilled to see someone I know personally, let alone my own flesh-and-blood niece, reporting on such weighty events. But, sweetheart, the real icing on the cake would be news this year of your engagement. Traveling to foreign locales is all well and good but it doesn't take the place of husband and home.

Sincerely, Uncle Leon

The Vomitron

Living in Moscow as a CNN correspondent in the 1990s was a completely different experience from living there as the impoverished young wife of a Soviet citizen in the 1980s. I had a BMW. I never rode the metro. I always shopped in the hard-currency stores, spending my dollars on meat imported from Finland instead of lining up for the shoe leather that they called meat in the domestic stores. My clothes were bought during vacations to Italy. Instead of trudging through the snow to a Laundromat that seemed to eat as many clothes as it cleaned, I had a maid. Just like the natives, I learned to be a capitalist in the new Russia.

By 1992, Boris Yeltsin was dismantling the unwieldy old arms of the Soviet state with a sledgehammer. But it was an enormous task, and Russia was not converted to a market system overnight. Instead there was an unpredictable mix of new and old. Kiosks and chaotic street markets sprang up in the open air, while old state-run businesses still occupied space within buildings. Vigorous entrepreneurs struck up bizarre alliances with old-style tenants to sell their wares. In one of my favorite examples, the main state-run bookstore on Gorky Street, now called Tverskaya Street, was doubling as a dealership for Chevrolets. The shelves of books seemed to lend credibility to the car salesmen's pitch. A customer might have come in looking for a Chevy coupe, and leave instead with Turgenev's collected works or vice versa. Such was the new Russia. The Lenin Museum rented out a floor to a modeling agency. In another wing, home appliances were on offer next to a museum display case featuring a lock of Lenin's hair.

A lot of Russians, denigrating the old methods that had held their nation together for decades, flung open the door to the outside world. It was often the tawdriest and most base that came first. Hustlers and modern-day carpetbaggers had a field day. Just as a vulnerable and needy woman welcomes the attentions of any man, including a scoundrel, an insecure Russia gobbled up the worst of the West.

Trevor was a refugee from New York's financial district. He had come to Russia looking for adventure, and he quickly saw the business potential that lay in a system newly opened to entrepreneurs and without much effective government regulation. Originally he had wanted to negotiate with the Russian Space Agency to take him up on a ride into space, but the Russians kept raising the price on him, even after he agreed to pay more than $1 million, so the plan never materialized. But he got to know MiG test pilots and quickly improvised a scheme to borrow MiG fighter jets from the Russian air force and take paying tourists from the West on expensive joyrides. MiG flights were a good diversion for bored drones from Wall Street with too much discretionary income. The Russian test pilots, just like everybody else in Moscow, were desperate for cash.

Everything could be bought or rented for a price. One day I was sent to do a story on Trevor. I went reluctantly: he sounded like one more foreign jerk taking advantage of the giant fire sale under way in Russia.

I arrived with my camera crew at the crack of dawn at Zhukovsky Air Base outside of Moscow with our special-clearance passes from the KGB, which we needed to get into this once-top-secret facility. My cameraman was Hugh, a six-foot-seven-inch Australian. I loved working with him because he had an eye for the absurd, and examples of absurdity abounded in Russia. His height was sometimes helpful: occasionally it intimidated people who got in our way, or it enabled him to reach above the crowd for a good angle. At other times it brought too much attention to us. Sergei, a Russian sound technician, was also with us. Between Hugh's wry sense of humor and Sergei's ability to mimic, I was laughing on most days.

When we arrived Trevor had his first customers in tow: a New York currency broker in her thirties and a somewhat elderly CPA from Wisconsin whose lifelong dream was to fly a fighter jet. The Russians insisted on a full medical checkup before flight.

"This should be good," I said, nudging Hugh to keep his eye on the seventy-five-year-old, who was about to be strapped to the heart monitor.

"Won't the g-force be enough to stop this guy's heart?" I whispered to Trevor, already imagining a potential headline: GREEDY ENTREPRENEUR KILLS UNSUSPECTING AMERICAN TOURIST BY IGNORING MEDICAL REGULATIONS.

The Russian technicians put the old man through several tests, and then one pulled Trevor aside to say he could not fly. A flash of green exchanged hands, and suddenly the old guy was deemed sturdy enough for the flight after all. The willing victims were suited up in Soviet-issue flight suits and given a few moments of instruction on how to bail out in case of emergency. Then they climbed aboard their respective MiGs.

Russian pilots are among the best in the world, but my confidence wavered when one couldn't get the canopy of his cockpit to shut properly. Luckily, he found a thick rubber band to hold it down. Trevor fumed when he saw that Hugh was zeroing his camera in on the pilot's repeated attempts to shut the cockpit, capturing all the most embarrassing and decidedly low-tech aspects of the ride. But the flight went well, and everyone survived. I got a good story out of it. I also got Trevor.

Trevor was American, but he was brought up all over the world and had cultivated a sense of bravado about making his way in foreign lands that was seductive. He was more appealing to me than your average Russian mobster draped in gold chains and tattoos, the kind of men I saw in the gym. Since Alessio and I had broken up six months before, I had been out on only one date, with an aggressive Russian businessman who was pursuing me. He turned up with three cars: a brand-new Mercedes sports car for us and two Volvos full of machine gun–toting bodyguards to follow. I already had to worry about getting shot on the job. I wanted a break while on a date.

So when Trevor came along, he looked pretty good. He was handsome, albeit in a Ken-doll way. He had dark features, piercing, thick-lashed eyes, and his most striking feature was a perennially deep tan he nurtured, even in Moscow's winter. I should have known when his own sister warned me off him that there would be trouble. But he was dashing and clever. He was also enthralled with Russia, and a relentless action junkie. On one date, we went on a ride in a MiG fighter plane. Another time it was a tour of a nuclear silo. Instead of a holiday snorkeling in the Virgin Islands, he wanted to take an icebreaker to one of the poles or visit bombed-out Beirut. Instead of being intimidated by my job, like most men I encountered, he thrived on it. He was always a willing participant and wanted to come along to whatever I was sent to cover. On our first date I invited him to the Pavletsky railway station. We were shooting a story on a group of French doctors who had set up shop in the squalid station to treat the homeless at night.

As Hugh, the cameraman, and I descended into the bowels of the station late that night, it was teeming with misery. Children tugged at us, begging for gum, money, a pen, anything. Mothers were camped out with hungry-looking toddlers and screaming babies, staring vacantly at us, not even bothering to ask for help. I was immersed in this kind of scene so often, I did not let myself feel the human misery that surrounded me: I kept focused on a task, taking notes. Trevor followed us around as we filmed old men with gaping wounds and Azerbaijani children with open sores being tended by the French doctors. The homeless lined up with gangrene and lice. With the Soviet Union unraveling, Moscow's train station was overflowing with the unwanted, the underbelly of Soviet society, swept out of sight for so long by the authorities. Now they were pouring into Moscow, often fleeing the former Soviet republics, many of which were now independent and mired in civil war. It was all in a day's work for me, and I was impressed to see Trevor, the devout capitalist, still tagging along.

"Dinner?" I asked.

"Just let me go home and throw up first," he answered.

A few nights later, Trevor called when I was getting ready to leave the office to cover a victory party for Vladimir Zhirinovsky, the rabid nationalist and anti-Semite who had unexpectedly won big in parliamentary elections. Trevor, always interested in meeting new people, asked to come. I gave him the address in a hurry, assuming that he would never find his way there, especially as he didn't speak Russian. But when my crew and I arrived, Trevor was already inside drinking vodka and making toasts with the Zhirinovsky clan. He knew how to have a good time. He once described himself to me as a soulless jumble of neurological impulses, but I thought he was the best pursuer of adventure I had ever met.

At one point, Trevor made a deal with Russia's Space Agency to take tourists for rides in their weightlessness-training plane. After collecting a few thousand dollars each from a group of thrill-seekers, we headed off to Star City, Russia's main space center. There are only five planes in the world that can simulate zero gravity in order to train astronauts for space, one in the United States, one in Europe, and three in Russia. Trevor rented one for the day. We were shepherded past statues of Yuri Gagarin and other Soviet space heroes into a classroom to watch a video explaining what we were about to experience. It was basically twenty minutes of people throwing up from the effects of weightlessness. Trevor had a word with our hosts about perhaps developing a better videotape. We were then given a five-minute instruction on how to use a parachute before being herded off for our adventure. The giant cargo plane, which we dubbed the "Vomitron" after the video, looks like a converted gym with padded walls and ceiling. We took off and flew to a high altitude at which the plane dipped, flying straight down, then pulled back up quickly in a parabola, creating zero gravity for about thirty seconds. It was the most disorienting and liberating sensation I've ever had. Like many people, I have flown in my dreams for years, gliding over meadows and trees, but now I was doing it awake, flying from one end of the plane to the other, spinning around in midair curled up in a ball. I felt giddy and thrilled and free.

Maybe the thing Trevor and I liked most about each other was our joint eagerness to try anything in Russia, this giant playground devoid of rules where we could feel like children. We relished the absurdities of daily existence in the new Russia. There were new adventures every day. My eternal hunt for a good story for CNN gave me license to seek out some of the wackier sides of what was going on. One day I visited the Lenin Brain Institute, where scientists had cut Lenin's brain into thirty thousand slices and for more than a century looked for evidence of his brilliance, only to discover that its capacity was no better than the average bus driver's brain. On another day I covered the Red Army Choir as they expanded their repertoire past the old limits of military tunes to include Frank Sinatra and Rolling Stones songs. Their brass version of "It's Only Rock 'n' Roll" in full military garb epitomized the often ridiculous results of Russia's efforts to transform itself. Russia's first gay bar opened up, with a giant fish tank where naked ballet dancers from the Bolshoi swam and performed an underwater dance. We also visited a new sex club catering to the gangster class that was located inside the foreign ministry's press center, where press briefings were held by day, and more nefarious activities occurred at night. As part of Russia's giant identity crisis, Moscow had become the capital of incongruous pairings, and Trevor and I explored it together.

Not long after we started dating, Trevor informed me that his ex-girlfriend back in Florida, a blond aerobics instructor, wasn't really all that ex. Trying to justify his sexual dalliances, he compared himself to a sports car.

"If you want to drive a Ferrari, with all the excitement and speed and craftsmanship, you have to put up with some quirks," Trevor said. "If you want reliability and comfort, get a Volvo."

Rather than realizing that Trevor was not the man for me, I blamed myself, looking for my own faults, as women often do.

Maybe I was too fat, I thought, so I dieted. Maybe I was too flabby, I thought, so I hired an ex–Olympic wrestling champion as my personal trainer. I got blonder. But nothing seemed to divert Trevor's attention away from my brain to my body. In my smarter moments, I thought about shopping for a Volvo. Unfortunately, those moments passed. I slipped back into accepting an unsatisfactory reality.

Then Trevor told me the "ex-girlfriend" was coming to visit him for Christmas. The trip had been planned before we had met, he explained, and he promised to use this occasion to break up with her for good.

I was accustomed to bad Christmas holidays. Christmas was always hard when I was growing up. A feeling of dread creeps into me around mid-December each year. We never had a tree, but not because my father was Jewish; my Protestant mother objected because it was a German tradition, and she would have nothing German around because of the fierce prejudice she had adopted during the war. No Krups appliances, no Volkswagens, and no Christmas trees. "They built the gas chambers," she often reminded us. With money short, we often received our presents a few days late. Christmas was put on hold till after the post-Christmas sales. I was full of expectations, pumped up by the endless commercialization of Christmas on television and by the excitement of other families I knew, but almost every year I felt let down. The disappointment felt painfully familiar when Trevor told me he would be unavailable during Christmas.

I didn't get much of a chance to worry about it. On Christmas Eve, thirty schoolchildren were taken hostage by a gang of Chechens who demanded a million-dollar ransom. I was soon on an Aeroflot flight south toward Chechnya, a mountainous region known for its black-market trading. We arrived at Rostov-on-Don, a southern Russian town near Chechnya, where the kidnapping had taken place. Armed with submachine guns and hand grenades, the gunmen had burst into a school and grabbed the children. They bundled them into a helicopter, and police gave chase through the Caucasus Mountains. We arrived at the school, where the parents had been waiting for twenty-four hours for news about their abducted children. They were distraught and terrified. After interviewing them, I sat outside the room to write my story. But every time I looked up at the worried, tearstained faces of these parents, I wanted to cry.

The kidnapping was over quickly. Russia's alpha forces, a special crack military unit, cornered the gunmen in the hills and retrieved the children safely: they were home in plenty of time for Russian Orthodox Christmas, celebrated in January. My crew and I were ready to fly back to Moscow, but all flights were canceled due to heavy snow. I wasn't sure when I'd be home. Then I spotted some of the tough-looking alpha soldiers hanging around the Rostov-on-Don departure lounge. Clearly their plane was going to take off. I found the commander and begged and pleaded to hitch a ride with the only plane dumb enough to fly anywhere in such conditions. I was told I would be allowed on as long as I swore not to talk to anyone. I agreed. But after a little vodka, the reserve of the gentle brute seated next to me, with hands the size of suitcases, broke down enough for us to discuss Tolstoy.

While I was pursuing Chechen hostage-takers through the Caucasus Mountains, Trevor was still entertaining his female visitor. My kitchen cabinet of personal advisers—my two sisters and my friend Lori—were soon united against Trevor. Alexandra, the first one to actually meet him during a visit to Moscow, formed a "Hate

Trevor" committee and took every opportunity to tell me how wrong for me he was. When I wouldn't listen, she would get Lori on my case. They were appalled at the depths to which I was sinking in order to please him. "Where's your self-esteem?" Lori asked during one of our many late-night transatlantic calls. Low self-esteem is an underestimated human affliction. It clogs emotional arteries, constantly nagging and belittling and dragging you down, no matter how accomplished the rest of the world thinks you are.

"Why do you give him so much power over you?" Lori prodded as I defended him. "If he hasn't come around in three months, you've got to purge him. Slash and burn. You are thirty-three and don't have time to waste on guys who can't go the distance." Lori was being practical. I wanted some sympathy. I dialed Francesca in Delaware.

"Why is it all the creeps are attracted to me?" I asked my younger sister.

"Because you'll actually talk to them," she said. "Most women wouldn't give them the time of day."

"I'm going to end up like Uncle Leon," I groaned. "Will you visit me when I'm living alone in a Jewish old-age home in Philadelphia?"

"Only if you serve me cherry Manischewitz wine like Uncle Leon always does," Francesca said. She had made the trek to visit Uncle Leon several times; I had yet to summon up the courage. Maybe it was because I feared I would end up alone too. Judging from his letters reminding me that a woman's life is not complete without a man, the same thought must have haunted him.

When I eventually visited Uncle Leon I saw that his main wall decoration is a minishrine to me, with newspaper clippings about CNN and a photo I once sent him of Boris Yeltsin and me. There is another in which I was interviewing King Hussein. He even has a picture of me with Richard Nixon in Moscow, although he is a devout Democrat. I always know he will be home when I call because he leaves only to mail his letters or to go to Tiffany's, a diner down the street. His weekly treat is having his favorite dish, chicken cacciatore, at the same time, five forty-five, every Sunday evening.

Uncle Leon has worn the same felt hat and tattered overcoat since I was a child. They are both relics of the 1950s. Whenever I picture him in this outfit he reminds me of Gogol's character Akaky Akakievich, who is so attached to his threadbare overcoat he comes back to haunt St. Petersburg in it. Uncle Leon always turned up at my mother's house in New Jersey with a brown leather overnight bag clutched in both hands. It was full of pertinent documents he had collected for me, some newspaper clippings about Ted Turner and CNN or a carefully written index card with his address in case I'd lost it, plus an empty one for whatever my new address might be. Uncle Leon is obsessed with address changes. He wrote to warn me two years ahead of my mother's scheduled New Jersey zip code change, then sent letters every six months in advance of the change to remind me.

Dear Siobhan,

I was pleased and delighted to catch you on CNN in recent days. I particularly enjoyed your report from Gilbraltar, especially your description of the Spanish attempts to gain a dominant stance in the area's political picture. Apparently the British intend to maintain the status quo. As proud as I am of your career, sweetheart, I would be remiss in my duties as an uncle if I didn't mention how important a girl's social life is and ultimately a successful marriage.

Now to the main point of my letter. In case you misplaced my previous letters to you, the following zip code change will take effect in your mother's area as of December. I have enclosed a clipping from the Philadelphia Inquirer *informing the public of this information.*

Affectionately,
Uncle Leon

His connections to others are few, so he holds on to them tenaciously, fearing those he loves might disappear out of his life if he isn't diligent enough to keep track of them. He always found me and kept those letters of encouragement coming to whatever corner of the earth I happened to be in.

So, because I did not want to fulfill my own prophecy or disappoint Uncle Leon in his main message to me, *find a man,* I soldiered on, and decided to give Trevor one more chance. Moscow can be a very lonely place for a single woman, and the selection of men was not much better than the food. After long enough in Moscow, turnips looked tempting. It's all about perspective. I made excuses and stayed with Trevor for another year. It took another war to knock some sense into me.

8

Dancing Warriors

In late 1994, events drew me to back to Chechnya. In this moun-tainous area of southern Russia, dissent against Moscow had been bubbling for years. Although the Soviet Union's dissolution had allowed the former republics to become independent, Chechnya was not a separate republic, but rather a part of Russia. Yeltsin felt that letting Chechnya go could threaten the integrity of the remain-ing Russian Federation by encouraging other ethnic populations to go their own way. While Chechnya was technically part of Russia, many Russians believed it was inhabited by an inferior race, a Mus-lim one at that. Chechnya was known in Russia as a bastion of gang-sters, arms dealers, and thieves, and incidents like hostage taking were common. Russians still refer to Chechens as *chernoi,* or black. The capital of Chechnya is Grozny, which means "terrible" in Rus-sian. It was aptly named: it looked medieval, with signs of modern thievery. Many of the streets were mud, and livestock jostled with

Cadillacs, while ordinary men carried knives in their belts. The arms bazaar was just down the road from the open-air vegetable stalls, and customers haggled over rocket launchers or Kalashnikovs as casually as if they were cabbages and carrots. The irony was, the Chechens were getting most of the arms from the Russian soldiers they were gearing up to fight, trading bottles of vodka or food for their Kalashnikovs. This kind of barter arrangement went on even during the height of the fighting. Desperate Russian soldiers would give their enemy arms to kill them with in exchange for a bottle of vodka.

I could understand that kind of behavior. I had handed Trevor a blueprint of my own vulnerabilities, practically an instruction manual on how to inflict hurt, in exchange for the possibility of love.

For more than three hundred years Chechnya had been a problem for Moscow. Stalin, himself from the Caucasus, felt that only ruthlessness would vanquish the Chechen spirit. After the Second World War, he accused them of being Nazi sympathizers and deported them all, banishing the entire population to Central Asia. Where there are no people, Stalin figured, there are no problems. When Nikita Khrushchev came to power after Stalin's death in 1953, he allowed the Chechens to return to their ancestral homeland, but this did little to allay Chechen distrust of Russia. Nestled in the Caucasus Mountains, far from the capital in Moscow, Chechens retained their distinctive culture. They still lived with a medieval clan structure dictated by blood vengeance and village elders. Weapons and honor were a way of life, and there were plenty of willing martyrs ready to take up the fight against Russian soldiers. In December 1994, when rebel Chechens actually declared independence, Yeltsin reacted as the czars did throughout Russian history: with brute force. It was war, one of the messiest wars I ever saw. It was the last place I wanted to go in the dead of winter. But I went anyway, unable to say no.

. . .

I made my way south with a crew. Alessio, with whom I still managed to work well, was the producer. Paul, from the Berlin bureau, was the cameraman; Sergei was our Russian soundman. We flew to Dagestan, a city in a neighboring province, since the airport in Grozny was closed. We hunted for a taxi willing to drive us to Grozny, but found only one Chechen driver prepared to risk the trip in his beat-up old Volga sedan.

As we approached Grozny, we were stopped several times by ragtag bands of Chechen thugs or guerrilla freedom fighters dressed in woolly sheepskin hats and heavily armed. Sergei kept quiet, since being Russian wasn't something to advertise. The Chechens were glad to see us, knowing that the press generally does well by underdogs. Almost instantly I felt plunged into a different century—maybe a past one, or maybe the future, like those *Mad Max* films that depict a postnuclear world. Groups of wild-eyed people were crouched around big, boiling cauldrons of foul-smelling sheep grease. There was a tolerance for brutality I had never seen before, a toughness built in by the harshness of daily life. The men would dance in a circle, chanting songs about their willingness to die a martyr. We called them the dancing warriors.

The buildings were crumbling and deserted. I turned to Alessio and asked, "Is this just usual Soviet disrepair or has there been fighting here?" We laughed nervously. In the disarray of the former Soviet Union, it was sometimes hard to tell the difference. We set up our editing equipment and work space at what was left of the hotel in the center of town. There had been no water for weeks, so one could smell the communal toilets from miles off. The windows had all been broken, and the cold and snow swept through the building. We used some gaffer tape to keep some of the icy wind from whipping through the room we shared. We might as well have slept outdoors and lessened the aroma from the bathrooms. If the cold or the stench didn't keep me awake, it was fear. The Chechen rebels had a big arms cache in the hotel's conference room, making it a serious target for the Russian army. Although trying to predict who or what would be a target was always futile. Civil wars are so chaotic that you can predict nothing. It's all about luck.

The Russians were so badly informed about the situation in Chechnya that when they carpet-bombed Grozny, they didn't realize that they were killing other Russians, or maybe they were just indifferent. Most of the Chechen population had already fled Grozny, going up into the hills to stay with relatives. The ethnic Russians who lived in Chechnya were still in the city, without people in the hills to escape to, so when the five-hundred-pound bombs dropped indiscriminately from ten thousand feet, it was Russians killing Russians.

Russian fighter planes made daily sorties into the city, dropping bombs from a high altitude to avoid Chechen antiaircraft guns. Alessio wanted us to sleep in the city center to provide constant live reporting Edward R. Murrow–style while under bombardment. I thought that was too dangerous: better if we moved back and made our base on the outskirts of town, driving in every day to report and therefore minimizing our exposure to the bombs, which were highly inaccurate. Almost ten years older than Alessio, I had a more developed sense of my mortality.

We moved out of the dilapidated hotel and into an evacuated kindergarten outside of town for some measure of safety. It was already full of media from all over the world, and the children's playground had been transformed into a satellite transmission station with huge dishes dwarfing the swing sets and slides. To cover the action in Grozny, we drove for two hours on icy roads in a

Soviet-made Lada car with bald tires. The ride worried me as much as the bombing raids, especially when one day we skidded into an oncoming truck. We weren't hurt, but it was a terrifying reminder of the danger we faced. I hadn't seen it coming because I worked during our bumpy journeys. I sat in the backseat with the camera in my lap and my eyes glued to the viewfinder. I watched our tapes and strained to hear the interviews, taking notes and trying to work out the story. I usually had the script mostly written by the time we got back to the work space so we could start editing it immediately, although the process was often slowed by power cuts. Getting a two-minute news story out to the world was generally an eighteen- to twenty-hour process between the driving, filming, editing, and electricity blackouts.

We were dependent on finding Chechens willing to drive us around in their cars, just to try to see what was going on. We lost drivers almost every day. One left us because his brother was shot. Another turned up with shrapnel wounds in his leg and I had to order him to go home. Finally we found one, Ahmed, who was fearless and reliable. Only trouble was, he couldn't take instruction from a woman, so I had to relay all communication through Alessio or Sergei. He also snored loudly, a problem in our communal sleeping arrangements.

The kindergarten was a small refuge against the considerable danger outside. We slept in tiny cots all together in an abandoned classroom. We wrote and edited at tables and chairs meant for five-year-olds. The tiny chairs upset me. I knew that the scenes we were writing about threatened the future of their usual occupants. Their lives and their psyches would be scarred forever by what they were witnessing now. I struggled to find the right words to give meaning to what I was seeing. I hoped, mostly in vain, that reporting on this desperate situation would somehow help improve it. Always under a deadline, I wished I had more time to craft the story in a way that might make a difference, however small.

Food was so scarce that our Moscow bureau sent a car on a treacherous thirty-six-hour drive just to bring us food. The day it was supposed to arrive, we learned that a journalist had been shot at a checkpoint. The car hadn't slowed down quickly enough and a Russian soldier had fired at it, killing a passenger. We just heard sketchy rumors for a few hours and I feared it was our car of supplies. I couldn't help thinking that I had helped cause a death because I was hungry. Our car arrived safely a little while later, but it was of little comfort to learn the identity of the German journalist who had died.

We lived like animals, the way most people live in a war. We didn't wash our hair for weeks. We had to squat to relieve ourselves wherever we could in the subzero temperatures, in bombed-out buildings or on the roadside. We managed only a few hours' sleep a day. We ate chocolate bars or crackers, or whatever we could carry with us in our pockets, surviving for days without a real meal. But we were under pressure to "feed" the network twenty-four hours a day. It seemed that there was no news to speak of in the rest of the world, so our producers were extra hungry for news from Chechnya. And our pictures were riveting. Journalists don't often get such graphic pictures of warfare: close-up shots of helicopter gunships and tanks firing; triage on the front lines. The network's thirst was unquenchable, never able to drink enough from the trough of human suffering.

I woke up each morning with dread. I was exhausted. My clothes were filthy. I knew I smelled. When Christmas Eve came, I was depressed. It was my worst Christmas ever. That night I felt determined to do something mad to remind me that there was a sane world outside this one. I hooked up one of our suitcase-sized satellite phones, generally used for news emergencies, and called L.L. Bean. At twenty dollars a minute, the American operator put me on hold and then wanted me to call back because the line was bad. I yelled at her, fumbling in the dark for a flashlight to read off my credit card number so that I could order a teddy bear as a present for my first nephew, Alexandra's son. I needed to feel some connection to this new life, however distant.

One day during our drive into Grozny, we came upon a grisly scene: a shopping street had just been hit by Russian bombers. It was next to a bridge, which must have been what the planes had been aiming at. The bombers might have missed their target but they succeeded in their general mission of causing terror and panic. Several civilians were killed and everyone was running away, searching for shelter. But when bombs fall from above, nowhere feels like shelter, and you feel as vulnerable as a scurrying ant. It is a helpless feeling, much worse than being fired on from the ground. By now our cameraman had gone back to Berlin, and had been replaced by a woman, Mary. She was about five-foot-two, skinny, and fearless. We went closer to survey the damage. Bodies were scattered in the packed snow, which was stained with blood and soot. Life had stopped in an instant. A woman still clutching her shopping bag lay motionless, her head no longer attached. A burly, mustached man was slumped over the wheel of his car, no longer hearing the wail of the horn. Fires raged in the snowy wreckage of people's homes nearby. If I survived this day, I promised myself, I would never sleepwalk through another day in my life.

I told Mary that if we had enough footage, we should leave. The Russian bombers had missed the bridge the first time, but they might come back. Just then we heard the sound of planes headed for us. My camerawoman was still thinking about getting that perfect shot, and did not want to move. I knew what was going on. A strange thing happens when you look through a camera lens. The images so vivid to the naked eye are in fact black-and-white to the cameraman, somehow muting their impact. Just as we are numbed by the violence we see on television nightly, the photographers, intent on collecting their images, are severed emotionally from what they see. When they look through their viewfinders, they forget that they are just as vulnerable as their subjects. I could see the blood. In an instant, I imagined my own body lying like a husk, shucked of its life. I pictured my hair matted with blood, and my family's horror when they got news of my death. I yelled at Mary to leave, but still she was reluctant; the pull of those dramatic pictures was too strong. Finally, I yanked on her arm and we ran for cover in a nearby building. The planes flew by, firing at other targets. Life-and-death decisions over a picture. We made them all the time. It seemed crazy. I was relieved to get out of there, thinking that I had beaten the odds one more time.

On that day, unbeknownst to me, my family came close to hearing of my death, as did my colleagues at CNN. A young American free-lance photographer named Cynthia Elbaum was killed as she took pictures of a bombing at another bridge. She was in her early twenties, experiencing her first war. As the news spread that an American woman had been killed, some Chechens who knew me and knew I was in the area guessed that I was the victim. They informed CNN in Moscow that I had been killed. The entire bureau went into shock and relayed the news to our headquarters in Atlanta. In addition to the horror of losing a colleague, our producers were in a dilemma. They were already reporting that a female TV correspondent had been killed, but they did not want to identify the victim as me until they informed my family in New Jersey. They called repeatedly but my mother was out. Meanwhile, as they reported that an unidentified American female journalist had been killed in Chechnya, any viewer who had been watching my daily reports from there could only guess that it was me, since I was not appearing on-air. After several hours of being out of touch, I called in from the satellite phone, and my producers were so ecstatic they put me on the air immediately, so that viewers would hear my voice and know I was alive. It was a strange feeling knowing that all my colleagues thought I was dead. But I had little time to contemplate, as we rushed back to the kindergarten to write and edit our story for the day.

For some correspondents, the thrill and danger of war becomes a way of life. Perhaps being near death makes them feel more alive. In Chechnya, I felt the opposite. I wanted to do my job well, but the shock of near-death made me ask myself what I was doing there. Was I emotionally disconnected? Was that why I could continue to operate in such a terrible environment? Maybe it was only my ability to abandon my feelings that allowed me to witness these horrors daily. I had somehow wandered off emotionally and psychologically, missing in action from myself. I suppose, in a way, this distance from my emotions made me a better reporter. I could act as a blank slate on which to convey other people's stories. But it also made me realize how much of me was dead inside. Going to Chechnya made me think, in the most basic way, that I deserved to live, and that I needed to inhabit my own emotional world instead of using news as a surrogate by stepping into other people's lives. I had to be bombed into valuing my life.

After that day on the bridge, I asked to be relieved in Chechnya and to go back to Moscow. I had been away almost a month, but it felt like far longer. It was a great relief to get home to my apartment in Moscow and soak in the bath for hours. But the relief was only temporary. I still had to file stories daily. And I knew I would soon have to return to Chechnya, because we were short of reporters who could go. I dreaded it.

And then the lure of the chase hooked me again. The Russian Defense Department granted a request I had put in weeks before, to spend time with the soldiers on the Russian side of the war. Despite my exhaustion and fear, I felt drawn to the chance, because it was the first access any Western journalist had been given to the Russian military in Chechnya. Reporting in any war can become one-sided. I empathized with the Chechen civilians who were being bombed, but it is often simply the side that is more accommodating to the media that gets the most sympathetic coverage. Almost all of the Western news was sympathetic to the Chechens, and I could understand why. Russian troops shot at our car when we first tried to approach them in Chechnya. But I still felt that the Russians deserved to have their side of the story told.

I headed south again on a Russian military transport plane, this time with another of CNN's powerhouse camerawomen, Cynde. We landed in a sea of mud, into which we plunged knee deep as we descended from the plane. Somehow we hauled our bags and cases of equipment through the mud to the building housing the military press department. We were at headquarters of the Russian forces in Mozdok, a dreary Russian town close to the Chechen border. We were there to persuade them to take us on one of their helicopters to the front lines in Grozny. Every morning we'd trudge onto the base past the same frozen dead dog lying in the snow outside the barracks. It bothered me. Couldn't somebody pick it up?

The misery of the Russian soldiers was nearly unbearable. Few of those we spoke to understood why they were there. Many were eighteen-year-old conscripts who barely knew how to use their

Kalashnikovs and wandered around looking dazed and shell-shocked. Outside the Russian camp, a crowd of women gathered each day—mothers, many of whom had traveled from far across Russia, looking for news of their missing sons. One officer said to me, "I've never seen anything like this in Afghanistan. This war is a meat grinder. We just keep throwing more boys at it and they get chewed up and spat out."

Cynde's and my persistence paid off. The Russian press officer, who had been so shocked to see two women get off the transport plane, held us off for days, promising to take us into the battle but not believing we really wanted to go. Even having gotten this far, part of me secretly hoped he would say no and I wouldn't have to go through with this. I was almost sorry when he eventually relented. We climbed aboard a postal helicopter that brought mail and other supplies to the front lines. The pilot told us to take off our flak jackets and sit on them because Chechens would be firing at us from the ground. I knew what it was like to be a helpless ant being bombarded from above; now I was going to get to feel the fear from the other side, like a duck in flight being pursued by hunters below. The pilots flew evasive maneuvers through the mountainous terrain. They were very skilled, but I had mixed feelings when I discovered that it was vodka that emboldened them. I think I held my breath for most of the trip. When we landed on a ridge where the Russians were dug in and heavily fortified with tanks and artillery, I felt safer. It was more secure to be taking pictures from the side, behind the big guns. We spent the day filming helicopter gunships strafing Grozny, and tanks and heavy artillery firing at the city. The hard part was knowing what was happening on the other side, to have seen the destruction each salvo causes. But the wounds were inflicted on both sides: at a makeshift triage tent, injured Russian soldiers were bandaged up to be quickly flown back to base; nearby a row of dead soldiers lay in the grass, stiff and lonely, no longer in a hurry. Moscow may have believed that holding on to Chechnya so as to not risk further disintegration of Russia was worth fighting for, but few of the soldiers on the front lines seemed to think so.

The war dragged on for months. The network's interest waned, then flared up again whenever the story heated up. People congratulated me when we were nominated for an Emmy award for our coverage, but I could not feel much joy in it. I never recovered from the brutality of my first month there. I never felt the same about Russia. I knew it was time for me to leave.

9

"Speaking to the Dead"

All her adult life, all my younger sister, Francesca, ever wanted was a husband and a baby. She never suffered from my wanderlust. She stayed close to home, satisfied with life's simple pleasures. I had to traverse the globe for years before the same thing looked attractive to me. While I went around the world, her longest journey was from New Jersey to Delaware. While I was covering other people's wars for a big broadcaster, she was working in a stable office, Xeroxing, stapling, and collating.

As different as we are, I feel an indescribable bond with Francesca. She is like my mirror. Our insides seem linked. She has a direct pipeline to my heart, often anticipating what I say or feel. The same things make us laugh and cry. There have been times when I have heard her voice on my answering machine and been confused: she sounds so much like me that I think the voice is mine. We have no inhibitions with each other. We share everything. I know she is always on my side. She brought fun and laughter into our heavy home. The longest relationship I will ever have is with my sisters—longer than with a spouse, my mother, or my child.

Francesca is one of the wisest people I know. She always knows where to look for answers, how to speak to her own heart for guidance. Though I was different, searching outside myself around the world, I came to value her kind of clarity and acceptance of a simpler life.

When we were children, my mother often teased Francesca by saying she would sell her to an Arab sheikh for her all-American blond, blue-eyed beauty. She did end up gravitating toward Middle Eastern men. They weren't confused by modern American gender issues and power struggles between the sexes, and took care of her in a traditional way. With them she could do what she wanted, which was to stay home, paint her nails, and take care of the house. She could play that role, which I knew I never could.

She eventually fell in love with a Lebanese man named Hadi, who worshiped her in his reserved and gentle way. They lived a suburban life: do-it-yourself projects on weekends, planning for their future brood. They were a funny pair. Always with his nose stuck in *The Economist,* Hadi was one of only a few people who asked me informed questions about whatever war I had just been covering. Francesca was more engrossed in the latest sitcoms, charming and witty in a way that she never needed to impress anyone with intellectual pretensions. Francesca's sorority-girl looks belie her wicked sense of humor and ability to mimic and have an entire room convulsing with laughter. Hadi played her straight man, a counterpoint to her antics. He was always supremely practical. They were saving and doing repairs on their house before they took the next step, marriage.

Not long after the war in Chechnya, Francesca called me in Moscow.

"Hadi came home from work today and I noticed a huge lump on his neck," she said. "He always reminded me of Daddy; I knew he'd get cancer."

I tried to calm her, pointing out that Hadi was only thirty-five years old, assuring her it was nothing that serious. But, as optimistic as I sounded, her news took my breath away. We had suffered through my father's cancer a long time ago as children, and I was terrified at the thought that she would have to go through that kind of trauma now, as an adult.

Eight months later Hadi was dead. It was the same cancer, lymphoma, that had killed my father twenty years before.

Francesca lost her man. She lost her house. She lost her dream of a happy family and children. Everything she had ever wanted evaporated in a matter of months. When I came to visit, I had been deeply moved by the love that I saw flowing between Francesca and Hadi as he lay emaciated in a cancer ward in Philadelphia, with only a few tufts of hair left. The tenderness between them was potent and wordless as Hadi gently drifted out of her world. One evening after I visited Francesca and Hadi in the hospital, I went home and read Kahlil Gibran. Their love seemed to embody his words. I cried and cried that night, for Hadi, for Francesca, for my father, for me.

For even as love crowns you, so shall he crucify you.
Even as he is for your growth, so is he for your pruning.
Even as he ascends to your height and caresses your
    tenderest branches that quiver in the sun,
So shall he descend to your roots and shake them in their cling-
    ing to the earth.

Hadi's cancer opened reservoirs of sadness I had been carrying around for two decades about my father's death. For everyone in my family, Hadi's death seemed to let us relive my father's death, since we were so young when it happened. My mother was practically inconsolable about Hadi, perhaps reliving sorrow she had had to suppress when my father died.

Just before Hadi's diagnosis, I took a trip to Barbados, the Caribbean paradise I had last seen just before my father died when I was fifteen. After I settled into a beachfront hotel full of British colonial charm and luxury, I went unannounced to see Janice, whose American sister I had been for two months. A small girl opened the door. She said her name was Siobhan. After I had left twenty years earlier, Janice and her sister made a deal that whoever had a girl first would name her after me. When Janice's sister gave birth, she kept the promise and named her Siobhan. Janice had two children of her own and, oddly enough, had given them Russian names, Natasha and Nicholas. It made me wonder at all our unconscious connections. Going back to Barbados felt like the beginning of the long road home that I needed to take, now that my Russian adventure was coming to a close.

With the irrational cruelty of Hadi's death and all the feelings about my father with which I was suddenly flooded, I sought solace on another plane of consciousness. I went to see a clairvoyant in London. She turned out to be a matronly blond Englishwoman who lived with her husband and children in plain row housing in a suburb outside London. I had expected a house full of candles and dark curtains, and instead found her husband watching a cricket match on TV in a perfectly normal sitting room, while his wife ushered me into the dining room to talk to the dead. She was recommended by a friend, and I was told she had given counsel to many members of the British upper class, including Sarah Ferguson, the

Duchess of York, according to the tabloids. She used no crystal balls or Ouija boards, but fondled my watch as she tried to make contact with the other world. She let me believe I could talk to my father, twenty years after his death. It made no difference to me whether it was real or not, whether I was talking to an actual ghost or an imagined one: it was a dialogue I needed to have. I wanted a chance to say things to my father that I had been unable to tell him before he died. I had never been able to say good-bye or tell him I loved him or feel his pride in me. I wanted him to know that I had turned out well, that I had graduated from Duke, and that I had taken graduate courses at Columbia, his alma mater, that I had a good job and that I spoke Russian. The process of talking to him made me feel as though I could finally let myself love him.

The more I talked to the memory of my father, the more I wanted to say. I wanted him to know that I had found our relatives in Russia. But there was a harrowing story behind that. Two cousins of my father, Boris and his sister Iveta, had corresponded with my father's family during the Second World War. In the mid-1950s, my father's family wrote to Boris and invited him to visit America, and suggested an alternative possibility of meeting one day in Israel. The letters from Boris stopped. All they got was silence. For years my father's sister, Rosalyn, was haunted by his disappearance, afraid that the one mention of Israel was enough to get Boris sent to the gulag. Now it was forty years later. Uncle Leon asked me in one of his many letters if I would try to find them, to put his sister's mind at ease. I used my reporter's skills and tracked down Boris and Iveta without much trouble. I was apprehensive about meeting them, afraid they might be bedraggled, bitter, and burdensome. To my delight, they were charming and warm. Although Boris had been expelled from the institute where he studied because of the letter from America, his career tarnished forever, he had rebounded well.

Despite his ordeal, Boris had become a linguist, speaking eleven languages, and was also an eminent economist at Moscow University. Iveta, a concert pianist, had masses of curly hair just like mine. Her husband was a polar explorer. Like their American cousins had done with my mother, they too seemed to ostracize Boris's non-Jewish wife. Although they welcomed me warmly to their home, I felt a tinge of rejection at not being quite Jewish enough.

Learning their history helped me understand my paternal family's terror of outsiders. It helped me understand too the kind of fear, to the point of paranoia, that existed in my father's family, and gave me an insight into why it must have been so hard for my father to break free of his own mother to be a proper parent to his children. Boris and Iveta filled out a lot of family history. My father's mother had come to America to escape the pogroms in Kiev. Her twin brother had been killed by a stone that was thrown through the window of their home by a rampaging crowd. Their mother was holding him in her arms at the time. For generations they had distrusted the outside world of non-Jews. In America that suspicion never waned, and my father's family never accepted me and my sisters into the family.

After Uncle Leon told his sister, Rosalyn, that I found our relatives in Russia, I told Leon that I wanted to meet her. She hadn't seen me or my sisters—her only nieces—since we were small children thirty years earlier. Her first words to me when we finally met were, "You have such Jewish eyes." I had mixed feelings about seeing her. I wanted not to like her. I had assumed she was an ogre. But she looked like my father, and my first sight of her linked me to him immediately. She was articulate and bright. She had curly hair. She had a dog. I liked her and felt slightly guilty that I did. Should I forgive her for ignoring us all those years?

When I spoke to my father through the psychic in London, I felt a message from him telling me to go to his grave. I had not been since his death. I didn't even know where it was. I had always worried it was unkempt and without a tombstone, that somehow he would be an embarrassment in death as he had been to me in life. The psychic drew a map, relaying instructions from my father, telling me which side of the cemetery, overlooking a hill, next to a tree. Francesca made fun of my willingness to listen to a psychic, but she promised to come with me the next time I came to America.

We got instructions from Uncle Leon on how to find the cemetery but had nothing but the makeshift map to guide us once we were inside the grounds. We found him easily; he was just where the woman who talked to the dead had described. His grave was simple. I brushed leaves off it gently, wanting to do something loving for him, to acknowledge him as important to me. We knew he had wanted to be buried next to his older brother, Norman, so we attached the ivy from my uncle's grave to my father's so the two brothers could be joined, just as my sister and I felt joined by our journey there.

IO

The Serb Side

I never paid much attention to the breakup of former Yugoslavia. Even though I was in the news business, I found coverage of the Balkans complicated and confusing. Besides, I had my hands full in Moscow. Then one day I was sent to Croatia. Suddenly I had to learn a lot in a hurry. When new borders were being drawn in ethnically mixed areas, large populations of Serbs found themselves in Croatia and vice versa, fueling a spiral of ethnic cleansing. One flash point was in Zagreb, the beautiful capital of Croatia, which in late 1995 was being shelled by the Serbs. The Croats had just retaken land lost to the Serbs during fighting in 1991 and driven the Serbs living there out of their homes. Now the Serbs had dug into the surrounding hills and were retaliating. A story I had thought little about was going to become very real, urgently real to me. That's the life of a reporter.

Atlanta had ordered us onto the next flight from Moscow to Trieste, Italy. I had to move so fast that I didn't have time to think carefully about what I was heading into, and what I would need to bring. I figured that nothing in the Balkans could be as brutal as what I'd been covering in Chechnya, so I suppressed the trickle of fear creeping into my belly and ran home to pack some things. Packing as a foreign correspondent can be a funny game. It always seemed that if I packed for two or three days, I'd end up staying away for a month. If I packed for a month, I'd be back in under a week. This time I took everything I had.

As soon as I landed in Trieste with my crew, we rented a van and drove into Croatia, about a five-hour drive. It was night when we crossed the border. I was bracing for a band of thugs to stop us at various checkpoints, with gun-toting goons drunkenly waving the butts of their rifles in our faces, the kind of unnerving thing I got used to in Chechnya. But we came to a normal border crossing with regular guards, who were even polite. We drove without incident into Zagreb, which surprised me with its cosmopolitan looks and charming buildings. The Esplanade Hotel, where we checked in, was full of old-world elegance.

The next morning, I was just starting to enjoy a glass brimming with fresh-squeezed orange juice, a delicacy that hadn't hit Moscow yet, when the peace was shattered by Serbs, who started lobbing cluster bombs into the city. The air-raid sirens were blaring, and ambulances went screeching past our hotel. We raced after them to capture the scene. It was chilling to see such a graceful European city under siege. Chechnya had seemed more suited to such savagery, where men with long beards still strutted around with sheathed knives, and where visitors like me were immersed in the daily horror without reprieve.

Here in Croatia, war was surreal. Well-dressed women shopping for the latest Italian fashions had to run for cover and crouch in alleys when shop windows suddenly shattered, splattering their finery with blood. It was shocking to see and report on, but as the days wore on I found especially strange the way we could observe and then pull back, going in and out of the action at will. We would go into the streets and cover the shelling, then return to our luxurious hotel for a bath or a sumptuous meal. As if we were stepping into a movie, we could shoot footage of carnage during the day, and leave when we had enough. We edited our footage in the comfort of a hotel, ordering room service. I could munch on a club sandwich while deciding which shot of a ransacked house or terrified refugee would work best in our story. This was "managed" war. I could cope with it far better than the constant, almost primal terror I felt in the more barbaric version of warfare under way in Chechnya.

I always thought of the United Nations as an ineffectual and bureaucratic organization, until I went to Croatia. Though UN forces were not exactly efficient, their presence clearly helped warring forces to exercise some restraint. UN officers often called us via cell phone to tell us where to find villages that were being retaken by the Croats. We would get onto a modern highway and, after stopping for a Coke and snacks at a gas station, turn off at the war exit and film the skirmish in full view of the UN monitors. Sometimes we stopped at UN compounds for lunch. We carefully checked out the nationality of the monitors. Nepalese curries were my favorite, although the Fijians had good food too. I thought if I spent time thinking about what we might eat, I could avoid thinking about what we might see.

I was grateful that only a limited amount of my day had to be spent in a war. I spent time at the underground mall across from the hotel, replenishing my wardrobe, which was still hard to do in Moscow. One day, as I went looking for shoes in the relative subterranean safety, I wondered if I had lost all sense of perspective. Or was I trying to delude myself into thinking I wasn't afraid? I was so used to lurching from one crisis to the next that I felt ill at ease sitting still. Had I chosen a daily dose of insanity to make sure my attention never wandered inward, to ensure that I only skimmed the surface of life? I had never planned to cover wars, but I was starting to realize that no matter how hard my job was, it seemed easier than confronting my own struggles. And yet covering other people's wars made me feel hollow inside. I tried to do something normal for myself every now and then, to remind myself that I existed as more than just a vehicle to relay someone else's story. One day I went for a manicure in the hotel. I felt deadened and hoped the touch of this woman rubbing cream into my dry skin would revive me. There was something inviolate in the beauty of perfect nails. Sometimes I went back to my room for a bubble bath while the city was under siege. I told myself it was OK to take twenty minutes off to soak in the tub and daydream, ignoring the shelling outside, but I always felt a nagging sense of guilt.

Coming into Croatia for the first time, I had to cram on the plane to catch up on the story. In general, Western news organizations saw the Serbs as the bad guys in the Balkans, since Serb forces there were clearly taking directions from Slobodan Milosevic, the Serb leader in Belgrade who was later demonized in 1999 for massacres in Kosovo. But I knew that there were two sides to every story. And this time Croats were retaking Krajina, a portion of land lost to the Serbs several years before, and conducting their own atrocities against Serbian civilians. Compared with other correspondents, I had a slightly different perspective, coming in from Moscow. The Serbs share the Orthodox Christian faith with their Slavic brethren in Russia, and many Russians believe that the Serbs, who suffered at the hands of Croatian fascists during the Second World War, are justified in behaving like bullies today. Russians also believe that the West blames the Serbs for all trouble in the Balkans, ignoring the vicious fighting engendered by Croats and Bosnians and Kosovars.

One morning we arrived at a village that had just been overrun by the enemy. It had that postnuclear look I had come to know in Chechnya: all the trappings of life were visible but life itself had been extinguished. There were no people stirring; only remnants of life lingered, lives left in a hurry. Photos were scattered on the ground; a child's toy lay where it had been dropped in the haste to flee. Dogs had been left chained in gardens to starve; their masters would never return for them. I needed to give them a chance at life, so I unleashed them when I could. Livestock wandered around dazed and hungry. Lives had been ransacked. In this case the victims were Serbs, chased out of their homes by Croatian forces. So I told their story. I described burned Serbian houses, lost Serbian lives. I interviewed a seventy-year-old Serbian grandmother whose painful history was etched into the deep lines of her face. She had survived Jesenovac, a Croatian-run concentration camp during the Second World War about seventy-five miles southeast of Zagreb. Serbs and gypsies were gassed and tortured there by Croatian forces collaborating with the Nazis. Serbs say hundreds of thousands perished, while Croats insist it was only sixty or seventy thousand. It is the kind of disputed memory that is at the heart of the hatred between Serbs and Croats and perpetuates the war in the Balkans. It is a rallying cry of Serb nationalism.

It wasn't easy to tell the Serb side. It was an unpopular side to tell. It is easier to relate a story with clear-cut good and bad rather than confuse people with explanations of what lay beneath Serb anger. Usually there is no black and white, especially when it comes to ethnic claims over land. I often felt a reflexive impulse to side with the one whose story was not being heard. And after the terrible reputation the Serbs had earned in Bosnia, I wanted to look at their side of the story when they were persecuted in Croatia. As a journalist, I often hope that showing both sides of a story will help resolve it. Only when all sides own up to their part in perpetuating conflict can reconciliation begin. Those who are being branded the bad guys often become even more frustrated as they sense that their views are not being heard.

It wasn't until later that I realized I might apply the same lessons to my own family. Maybe it was because I never learned my father's side of things that I felt so drawn to trying to understand the less popular views around the world.

Not long after covering Croatia, on a visit to the United States, I went to see Uncle Leon. I called a week in advance to tell him I was coming, because Uncle Leon doesn't like surprises. He was thrilled and decided we would go to his favorite haunt, the Tiffany Diner.

"I'll go right down there and make a reservation for us, sweetheart," he said.

"Do diners really take reservations?" I had to ask.

"Sweetheart, I'll make sure they do, because every moment we have together is precious and I know what a busy lady you are."

When I found myself sitting across from him in Tiffany's, eating my turkey meat loaf on white bread with mashed potatoes, something changed. I felt as if I were seeing Uncle Leon clearly for the first time, after years of thinking of him as part of the evil family that neglected us. Now I saw a kindhearted, open, loving man who just wanted for me all the things that had eluded him in life. For years I had accepted one version of events, never questioning my mother's interpretation of my father and his family. The reality was much more interesting.

In the past, whenever I had gone home to visit my mother's house, Uncle Leon came to see me, taking the train up from Philadelphia. It often felt like a chore to see him. Instead of taking in his devotion to and acceptance of me no matter what I did, I was ashamed of his old-world appearance and manner. Unconsciously I associated him with my father, the enemy camp. But that night at Tiffany's I looked at Uncle Leon through my own eyes. It was the first real conversation we had ever had, and I saw a person with a hard and painful past, but one who loved life and felt joy in its simple pleasures. It made me eager to hear stories about the family.

As one of three brothers, Leon could never fulfill his mother's dream—every Jewish mother's dream—of having a doctor for a son. "I couldn't cut the mustard, sweetheart," he said often. His elder brother had committed suicide while attending Cornell University. Once it was clear that Leon was never going to be a doctor either, my father, the youngest, was the last hope for a doctor in the family. The family had poured all their resources into getting him to medical school. When he returned from Belfast with a young Protestant wife and small children instead of a medical degree, his family was enraged. They felt he had let them all down, which led to all those years of neglect.

As for Leon, he had joined the Signal Corps after dropping out of law school. Three weeks before being shipped to Europe for D-Day he had a nervous breakdown. In those days, mental illness was handled harshly. He was given a year of shock treatment. "It felt as though they killed my brain repeatedly," he told me at Tiffany's that evening. "It took decades for my mind to heal." It broke my heart. Uncle Leon always wanted a normal life, a wife and children, but he found it hard to reach out and he remained single. Instead he rooted for my father and came to see us when his mother and sister would have nothing to do with us. He felt loyal to his little brother and he loved his nieces. "You should be proud of what a devoted uncle you have always been to us," I told him.

"My greatest regret was not having a family of my own, sweetheart, and I don't want to see the same fate befall you. It is my most ardent wish to see you married before I die."

"Believe me, it is my ardent wish to see me married someday soon too, Uncle Leon. I'm working on it, trust me."

The Spa War

I told myself over and over that it was time to get serious about finding a man to settle down with. But then military conflict would break out somewhere else, my producers at CNN would ask me to go, and I would say yes. When I was sent to Israel, I was intrigued. After Chechnya and then Croatia, covering warfare in Israel felt like a vacation.

Israel's northern border with Lebanon had been a flash point off and on over the years. Southern Lebanon had been a staging ground for the Syrian-backed Hezbollah guerrilla fighters who were fighting with Israel over the nine-mile stretch of Lebanon that the Israelis occupied. Cross-border fighting was common, but it had escalated in recent days. It was April of 1996. CNN decided to mobilize its own forces on the border.

When I arrived, it felt as though I had come to a spa. Qiryat Shemona was a popular Israeli resort town located in a lush oasis in the desert. The land was dotted with poppies, and the area was a popular hiking destination for Israelis. My crew and I slept in a comfortable hotel with clean sheets and room service. There were good restaurants and working telephones. The weather was divine—warm and sunny every day. It was strikingly civilized compared with the medieval brutality of Chechnya. The only thing that would remind me I wasn't on holiday was the sound of heavy artillery at night from the unit stationed on the hills above us, lobbing shells into southern Lebanon. In answer, an occasional Katysha rocket landed in town or the surrounding fields. I felt none of the terror of being under siege by a Russian aerial bombardment.

Warm wars are more tolerable than cold ones. I learned that the staff at CNN was divided sharply into those who would cover a cold-climate war and those who would go only to one in a warm climate. There are legions of cameramen and producers and correspondents who refuse to cover a military conflict of any kind unless the weather is warm enough for shorts. I came to this revelation too late in life.

In Israel, I got up early in the mornings to get some exercise with Elaine, a CNN editor. Despite the shelling, I felt glad to be able to exercise while on assignment, instead of succumbing to the usual neglect and junk food on the road. We worried about the wisdom of wandering around outside, with all the shelling that was going on, but reassured ourselves: "Those Syrians have terrible aim." Most of the town was in the air-raid shelters or had been evacuated. But there we were, doing our power walks through the hills, doing our best to ignore the rockets that fell occasionally in the pastures a few hundred yards away. For no rational reason, we felt sure they wouldn't hit us.

After a buffet breakfast, we often headed up to the Israeli artillery base to interview the soldiers who were firing their enormous guns after morning prayers, their rhythmic communion with God interrupted by the cannon fire. I felt safe with the Israelis. It seemed such a sanitized way to wage war—atop a hill, never seeing the enemy or the misery they caused on the other side of a ridge. Many soldiers would chat with their girlfriends on their cell phones from the battlefield. Like those soldiers, I didn't want to connect with the carnage on the other side.

There was none of the blank horror I'd see on the faces of Russia's conscripts: the Israeli soldiers believed in what they were doing. They were bred to. At one point I came upon a group of soldiers inscribing one of the shells, *To Sheikh Nasrallah, with love,* referring to the chief of the Hezbollah on the other side of the border. When I asked one young soldier what he felt about the bloodbath Israeli shells caused when they hit the UN compound full of refugees in the southern Lebanon security zone, he shrugged. "They are civilians," he said. "They are people too, and didn't do us any harm. But these things happen in war."

Uncle Leon was thrilled I was in Israel and he told me he was glued to the television. I often called to tell him just before I was on the air. "To think that a girl with Jewish blood is reporting on such a timely topic for Jews around the world." He said, "It makes me so proud, sweetheart. However, a crowning accomplishment would be news of your marriage." He was hoping, I'm sure, that I might find a nice Jewish boy in Israel. Instead I found Julian.

After several of weeks at the war, I got a call out of the blue from Julian, a friend of a friend. A British journalist based in Israel, he invited me for a drink when I came back through Jerusalem. I'd never met him but he had seen me around and insisted on meeting me. I was flattered. I was exhausted from weeks of eighteen-hour days covering the story. I needed some romantic excitement.

Julian was not my type. He was blond, and I liked dark men.

He was sort of chubby and chain-smoked cigarettes and had an English-schoolboy way about him. Yet he had been brought up in Africa, so he had an earthy, wild quality that was at odds with his exterior.

We felt an instant attraction to each other. We walked the ancient Jerusalem streets and talked of our sympathy for the Unabomber's disgust with the modern world. We discovered in each other an inclination toward Luddism. He understood my waning tolerance for the profession we shared. We exchanged confidences as we watched the religious Jews bobbing at the Wailing Wall, pressing their handwritten wishes into the crumbling stone edifice dividing the city between Arab and Jew. The desert heat and the mysticism of the place heightened my senses and helped stoke the passion that was intensifying between us by the minute. We wanted to devour each other, and before night fell and the muezzins' final call of the faithful to prayer, we raced up the two flights of stairs to his bed.

For seventy-two hours we made violent love. The days were a blur. There was nobody else in the world but us. He said I reminded him of a lioness he once saw on the African plains. His intensity smashed through the numbness I had been feeling. He told me a hundred times a day that I was beautiful. He read me poetry in the bath, and jumped up from the table at restaurants to kiss me. He revived me, giving me back life that had been sucked out of me on the battlefields of my daily world. It was intoxicating.

"You have been a hurricane in my life—blowing through with such amazing power and force and upsetting everything, leaving devastation in your wake," he said as I got on the flight back to Moscow. I was in tears.

By the time I got home, he had left five messages on my answering machine, each one more poetic than the last. "The state of my life mirrors the state of my bedroom—a sweet, mad energy has blasted through it, leaving lingering, delicious chaos behind. If only all the mess in this wicked world could be so sweet."

I felt dazed but happy. I had finally met someone like me, with a huge appetite for life and love. He called me constantly and spoke of how he wanted to have a tribal wedding in Kenya. We might have been together only a few days, but whatever we didn't know about each other, we let our imaginations fill in, feeding the fantasy. We were two people so hungry for a connection, we just stampeded into the dream of a perfect future together. A friend who knew us both admonished me not to take too seriously these relationships on the road. "This one has a reputation," she warned. I didn't listen; I didn't care. This was different, I thought, the real thing. He would change my world. We would run off and build a life together.

Then I got caught up in Russian elections, while he was busy with Israeli ones. As soon as the nuts and bolts of reality tightened, with the complications of living in two different countries, he became distant almost as fast as he had jumped in. I was devastated and tried too hard to cling. That made it worse. It ended almost as quickly as it had begun.

Lori tried to soothe me, even though she couldn't believe it, since this one had seemed so promising. She was, as ever, wise and practical. "Don't waste time pining over him; if he's not the one, move on," she counseled. "You have no time to waste." She was more concerned about my biological clock than I was.

Despite my disappointment, I allowed myself to see that at least I was getting better at choosing men. After Trevor's neglect, my affair with Julian helped rebuild my confidence that I was desirable and that it was not always my fault when things did not work out. Maybe Julian hadn't been ready for me. Maybe I had expected him to be something he wasn't ready to be. But I felt naive. Here I was, an experienced journalist, skilled at cutting a clear path through murky situations in war or politics, but love threw me. It was getting embarrassing, telling my friends and family about another new man who didn't work out.

"Don't be so desperate," said my mother. "You have a great life; what do you need to have everything for? Why do you need a man anyway? You have that incredible job, you travel the world, and you have Max for companionship. Who could want more?"

She was referring to my new canine friend. I always looked to my animals for clues as to how I was progressing with human relations. As my choice in canine company improved over the years, so did the men I attracted. Max was a big step up from Sara, the bloodhound, just as Julian was from Trevor.

Max was a gray-and-white Tibetan terrier, one of many well-bred dogs thrust into Moscow's streets: with the encroaching poverty caused by the reforms, many Russian families could barely feed themselves, let alone a dog. Many fine dogs were dumped in the apartment blocks where foreigners lived, since they would have a better chance of finding a home. Max had taken refuge that winter at the CNN bureau, another of Lena's strays. We tried in vain to find a home for him, and it seemed incredible that no one wanted him. He was such an adorable soul I couldn't bear the idea of turning him back out into the snowy streets.

My mother was coming for a visit in less than a month. She would never turn away a dog in need. I called her in New Jersey and asked her if she wanted to take back a homeless Tibetan terrier. She said yes without hesitation. Max became her obsession even before she met him. Until she arrived, he was almost all she talked about when I called.

"I bought a new bed for him," she said. "I've called the Tibetan

Terrier Society and they are sending me information about the breed. You know, they used to guard the Buddhist monasteries in Tibet."

She was evidently more excited about her new dog than about coming to see me in Russia. Only trouble was, by the time she arrived Max had been living with me and I was in love. I kept him for myself. She was heartbroken, and had to go back to New Jersey empty-handed.

"If only you could find someone like Max," she said unexpectedly, referring to my quest for a man. "Small and hairy and loyal." It was about the most intimate conversation we'd ever had about my love life.

My mother was right about one thing: men could probably smell my desperation. I badly wanted someone to walk into my life and take me away to a normal world where I'd have babies and bake cakes instead of traipsing through muddied fields littered with bodies of plane-crash victims. The world's misery was taking a toll on my soul. I was tired of being dropped into other people's tragic or profound moments. I was beginning to realize that I wanted to live some of my own.

Cyberdating from
the Front Lines

I had been in Moscow almost five years before I got my transfer to London in 1995. I had loved Russia deeply, obsessively, but I had been cut off from the rest of the world for so long and taxed by the difficulties of day-to-day life in Moscow. I knew it was time to make my life easier.

Moving to London was exhilarating. The royal family was at war, with Diana and Charles taking potshots at each other in the British media almost every day. CNN had an insatiable appetite for that soap opera, as well as for the unending trauma in Northern Ireland, where a yearlong cease-fire was crumbling. I seemed to have good luck with breaking news. My mother said that if I were sent to cover a dog show a riot would break out. In London I covered all kinds of stories, from IRA bombs exploding to eccentric old ladies who rescued donkeys from around the world to more plodding political analysis on Britain's position in the European Union.

Whenever news broke, I had to jump and become an "expert" in a matter of hours on any subject, whether it was the repatriation of stolen Nazi gold or Albania's economic crisis. I loved the range of stories and different people I met every day, from presidents to homeless drug addicts and everything in between.

Even Uncle Leon from afar could tell how good the change was for me.

Sweetheart,

It was a joy and delight to catch you on the television reporting on the recent bombing in London. You look much better since your posting to England. Apparently the English food must be preferable to that in Moscow. I hope this factor helps with your prospects of finding a suitable mate in the coming year.

Uncle Leon

Uncle Leon was right. I was ready for a man, and tired of the slim pickings in Russia. The advent of e-mail radically improved my prospects. At least, it broadened my geographical scope. I discovered that essentially I could date anyone from anywhere in the world, even though I was still on the front lines in different parts of Europe. It had the added advantage, as so many cyberdaters have found, of allowing me to get to know a date from the safe distance of cyberspace.

In London, my social life was still a disappointment. I had been so anxious to get away from Russian men that I never stopped to think what their British counterparts might be like. For the most part I found them inbred, pale, and wimpy. Many were unable to look me in the eye. Consider what Princess Diana had to go through with her quintessential British male. It soon became clear that there was nobody here for me.

Jordan, a Hollywood-producer friend who acted as my Jewish godfather, tried to help by launching his own search for me in Los Angeles. He felt indebted to me for showing him a good time when he had visited St. Petersburg with a group of filmmakers a few years earlier. I had snatched him away from his boring tour group and taken him to some of my favorite haunts, like Peter the Great's three-hundred-year-old collection of anatomical abnormalities, a grisly exhibit of deformed fetuses, two-headed lambs, and Siamese twins pickled in jars.

I started to get e-mail from men Jordan decided were desirable suitors. Looking back, I have to question whether that museum choice had given him a warped impression of whom I might be interested in. Still, these cyberdates brightened up many lonely nights I spent locked in a hotel in Albania because of a shoot-to-kill curfew, or trapped in Belfast waiting for the Irish to throw more petrol bombs at each other. My favorite cyberromance was with a Beverly Hills plastic surgeon.

SCREEN NAME: LKoplin
LOCATION: Beverly Hills
BIRTH DATE: 9/18/50
SEX: male
MARITAL STATUS: divorced (almost)
HOBBIES: family, friends, music, the Beatles, ragtime guitar, skiing, reading, learning, life
OCCUPATION: Plastic surgeon
PERSONAL QUOTE: "To love another person is to see the face of God."

Dear Siobhan,

I thought I'd start by sending you my AOL profile, which forced me to compress a lifetime into an obscenely short list. I understand you are doing some terrifically exciting stuff overseas and am very anxious to hear about your international life and times. My quote of the day (just the first half; if you like it more to follow):

"So through the eyes love attains the heart; for the eyes are the scouts of the heart, and the eyes go reconnoitering, for what it would please the heart to possess."

L

Dear L,

How brave to send a blind e-mail to some strange woman overseas. Loved the verses you sent me and would love another installment, although in our case it is not eyes but words in cyberspace that must do the reconnaissance. How very modern and old-fashioned at the same time to be courted by words alone.

I don't have a computer profile but I guess if things get bad enough and I resort to joining a computer dating service my profile would go something like this:

NAME: Siobhan (shi-von)
BORN: 10/10/59
HABITAT: airplanes, hotels in places nobody in their right mind wants to be
FAMILY: one Tibetan terrier (Max)

OCCUPATION: professional snoop, voyeur, troublemaker, storyteller, witness to man's genius and folly (TV reporter)
THINGS I LOVE: my family, friends, yoga, reading, writing, nature, walks, the ocean, animals of all kinds, Italy, food, epiphanies, scuba diving. (I like skiing too, and what I lack in style I make up for with a fearless approach to slopes.)
PERSONAL QUESTION: Wondering what almost divorced means. Is that A: getting divorced and the paperwork hasn't gone through yet, B: bored with wife, thinking about divorce, C: none of my business?

Look forward to hearing from you,
S

Dear S,

How thrilling to receive a message from a beautiful war correspondent flung far across the Atlantic Ocean.

I loved your computer profile. In getting my e-mail today there were two different e-mail ads for "How to get a date with a beautiful woman: what to say, how to get their phone number, how to build your self-confidence, and what conversation is appropriate on the first date." Well, now, let me tell you, as a guy newly released on the dating scene (more later) this seems kind of interesting to me. But then I realize, "Hey, wait, look who I'm writing to at this very moment!" So the messages were deleted. I did not order anything and will just have to wing it like the rest of us.

About your multiple-choice question, papers filed last fall, temporary settlement done, final terms of money and custody of children (I have two) is scheduled for December. Sounds very clinical but what lies at the deeper unspoken level is that the marriage is well over; we are living separate lives.

I like to be around people who love and appreciate nature, walk through it, touch it, smell it, and embrace it. I love people with big brains, full of interesting stories and facts, inquisitive and well-read. Even more fun if they get to write about it, share it with others: that's how we get to look inside each other, right?

Larry

Dear L,

Thanks for your honest answer to my somewhat impertinent question. Sounds like it's been a tough year. Speaking of people's insides, I've just spent the week at War School. It's a sort of survival course for war correspondents run by former SAS guys.

They operate pretty much as TV reporters do. Small mobile groups with no backup are dropped into hostile environments to gather information; only difference is they've been trained to survive and we just seem to know how to find trouble. I was looking forward to a relaxing week off work lolling about in the Welsh countryside but instead it was serious boot camp. We were shelled, shot at, forced to drag big bleeding bodies across muddy fields and stuff their fake oozing guts back inside them.

What has been really frightening about this is realizing how unprepared journalists generally are when they go into war zones. I feel 1000 percent more confident now knowing that I could actually stop someone's arterial bleeding instead of standing idly by and watching a colleague die in the field. How the hell did you survive medical school?

Besides general triage medicine they also taught us useful urban skills, like how to move a land mine or disarm a grenade. Never know when this could come in handy.

S

I started to think that this kind of cyberdating was much easier than having to wash my hair and get dressed and actually go out on a date. Tired after a day's work covering bombs or riots, I could at stay home in my pajamas and weed out the undesirables much more quickly. I could also get lost in a fantasy and avoid the real-life pitfalls.

Dear S,

Glad to hear you went to medical school, even if only for a few hours. I, for one, am very interested in moving a land mine, as I've never known anyone well versed in the subject. I wonder how difficult it must be for you to sustain any meaningful relationships when you are so often on the go, in dangerous locations. Exhilarating, yes, but a crimp on sharing a cup of coffee and croissant with an important person on a Sunday morning?

My dear Cyber Surgeon,

You raise a sore point. I have been privileged to see history-making events on a daily basis. What I see in a week, most won't see in a lifetime. But I have paid a heavy price in the relationship department. I have such constant input that nothing seems to sink in or get absorbed. I jot things down in my journals, fragments that I promise to make sense of later, epiphanies shoved down and forgotten as some new experience gets packed on top. I want to stop, stay still, and travel the rugged internal terrain. I'm tired of wars, riots, and other people's misery. I feel like hiding under my desk when news breaks so I don't have to cancel another dinner party or miss my yoga class.

S

It was oddly reassuring to think of this man, whose life was all about order, going to the same office every day and trying to chisel perfect-looking humans. My life was the opposite as I went out each day into chaos to expose humanity's flaws. His efforts at creating perfect noses and thighs seemed futile to me. I thought of moving to Beverly Hills and putting up a shingle next to his office, SOUL DOCTOR, capturing some of his customers as they emerged. Clearly their souls must have been hurting to need so much rearranging of their exteriors.

My cyberromance with Larry trundled along for a number of weeks. We even spoke on the phone once, but somehow the more disembodied he was, the better I liked him. In one of his e-mails, Larry quoted Dylan Thomas on the importance of defying death by living a big life. Days later, Princess Diana did just that.

When Diana's car crashed in Paris, the London bureau chief woke me up at one in the morning. I couldn't sense how huge a story it would become; perhaps no one could. All I felt was another intrusion in my life. I had to drag myself out of bed and figure out who was going to walk Max. I interrogated the taxi driver for his opinions on the way to the bureau.

"I'm stunned, love, just stunned," he said. "But running around with that playboy trustfunder with four Ferraris, I'm not surprised that she ended up in trouble." Taxi drivers were sometimes the only source I had time to talk to before being thrown on the set and turned into an expert on what the "people" thought. I knew the second I walked in the bureau that I would be live on television for endless hours answering questions to which I didn't always know the answer.

Interest in the Diana story was so intense that my producers put me on the air every fifteen minutes for updates, keeping me on standby for hours at a time. At first we were looking for anything concrete to report: reactions from Buckingham Palace, feelings of the people who came to drape flowers all over the gate outside, anything. Only after many hours of frantic reporting did I have a chance to take a breath and think about Diana's death. I had covered her closely for nearly a year, reporting when she went public about an affair, an eating disorder, her suicide attempts, her unhappiness in her marriage. The British media endlessly dissected her every utterance, some arguing that she was mentally unbalanced, while others found her openness refreshing.

Just about any woman who is plagued by low self-esteem, who worries about her weight, who has trouble with men, who tries to find herself at the gym or with psychic healers—any woman with everyday problems in the modern world—found a spokeswoman of sorts in Diana. She communicated an image of caring with which ordinary people could identify. She took her sons to McDonald's and to amusement parks. She was into aromatherapy. She was a woman loved by many but who still felt alone. I felt like a soul sister.

I stood outside Buckingham Palace doing live shots all day when she died. Before the sun rose we had set up a satellite truck to broadcast indefinitely. When the first trickle of people started bringing their flowers and grief to the gates, we had no idea that so many would eventually come that they would bury the gate in a mountain of flowers. They were all kinds, the quintessentially reserved English old ladies, new Labour businessmen, mothers with children. It was as if all the repressed emotions of centuries erupted on the streets that week. Diana's death was like a lightning rod for unresolved loss in this country. It was a chance for virtual grieving. All those who couldn't cry for their own hurts and losses joined in this communal torrent of sorrow.

I often called my mother when I was desperate for background information, since she was often quicker than getting information from CNN's library in Atlanta, which was hampered by the time difference. She is an expert on everything, with an innate predilection for accumulating knowledge. No matter how obscure the topic or location I called about, she always seemed to have something to tell me from her encyclopedic mind. Sometimes, being mortal, she puts the phone down to consult her Encyclopaedia Britannica, with me holding on in a hotel room in Ashkhabad or Tirana. Whatever she told me went from her mouth to ears around the world. When Diana died, it was my mother's finest hour. It was the middle of the night when I called desperate for something to say about Westminster Abbey, a rumored site for the funeral. My mother, from her bed, listed the poets and noblemen buried there and rattled off other fascinating details about obscure relations and protocol. Her knowledge of the royal family was vast. And what she didn't know, my stepfather, Tim, did.

My mother had remarried, this time to a man who had much in common with her. Tim, with his shaggy beard and curly gray hair, looks like Karl Marx and has socialist sensibilities to match. He is kindhearted and will do anything for anyone in need. One winter evening he arrived home barefoot, having given away his shoes to a homeless man. Another time he brought home an abandoned boy, John, whose drug-addict mother had left to live in the bus station in New York. John ended up living with Tim and my mother for a couple of years, along with his temperamental pet parrot, Iggy. Anyone who sat under the bird's cage was bombarded with bird shit or cherry pits. Both my mother and Tim loved birds and wildflowers and would spend hours walking and pointing out all manner of weeds to each other. Tim would bring back offerings from the woods to her. I came home one holiday to find a dead mole tucked away in the freezer as though asleep among the ice-cream cartons and coffee tins; another time a baby fox was in deep-frozen slumber, and a wasp's nest adorned the hallway. And, just like my mother, Tim is a voracious collector of facts. So with twenty-four-hour coverage of Diana, those two helped fill a lot of airtime on CNN.

Since my mother is British, she had her own opinions about Diana, and the least I could do, as a price for the instant reference library, was listen to her rant. She felt it inappropriate for Diana to have gallivanted in public, and to have aired the royal family's linen in such an aggressive way. She was also appalled by the outpouring of emotion after Diana's death. "I don't even recognize the British anymore, wailing in the streets like that," my mother said. She called it the "Oprah-ization" of the entire world. Americans were vulgar enough, with their feelings constantly on display, my mother felt, and now the British were becoming just as bad.

My mother disliked Diana for all the reasons I adored her. What I saw as an effort to know herself, my mother labeled self-indulgence. I thought baring her soul to her public improved her image. My mother branded it as weak and shameful, a kind of promiscuity of emotion. My mother is one of the most giving and caring people I know, doing anything for a complete stranger, rescuing the Bosnians or feeding the homeless. But, like many of her countrymen, she is more comfortable with other people's pain than her own.

My mother's disdain for emotion reflects her generation and culture. She was born late, to Victorian-era parents. My grandfather ran Belfast's poorhouses, orphanages, and hospitals. He often took his young daughter on his inspections, so concern for the underprivileged was drummed into her psyche from an early age. Her elder brother, Brian, joined the navy during the Second World War. When his ship, which was bringing supplies to the Soviets in Murmansk, was temporarily believed to have sunk, it was not discussed in my mother's family. Secrecy and tightly contained emotion were not just family traditions, they were part of the national character of the time.

On the day of Diana's state funeral, a week after her death, I was outside Westminster Abbey with a cameraman, Todd, with whom I had worked for years in Russia and in London. He is one of the few people in television news who understands where to draw the line between capturing human emotion and tragedy and allowing people their privacy. He is sensitive to one of the hardest parts of our job, which is sticking the camera in the faces of people in pain. I was always uncomfortable with this aspect of my job, feeling like an intruder. Diana's funeral was one of those rare moments when, as a journalist, I stopped observing, analyzing, and poking and instead got swept up in the moment. Todd put down his camera and I put away my notebook and together we wept with the bikers, punk rockers, old men, taxi drivers, and tourists who gathered in the streets. It felt good to share a glance or a hug or a tear with so many strangers who had let down their guard. It felt good to be part of the human race and not just an observer.

To me, Diana's death was also a resounding reminder not to drift through life. I had this coveted job and glamorous career, meeting world leaders and history makers regularly. But I often felt empty at the end of a day. The price was getting too high. I would go home each night to my elegant London apartment full of treasures I had collected from around the world. Max was always dutifully waiting for me, and pleased to see me, but it wasn't enough. I lay in bed at night, stroking his furry head, and wondered how I had ended up alone in my late thirties, with no family of my own. I wanted my own tribe, my own people. In Chechnya I saw that I had to get out of Russia to save my life. Now I knew I had to get out of reporting to save my soul.

The Orangemen

It was time to find a man and start a family. That phrase was becoming like a broken record in my head. But I found myself unable to quit. Every time I started to talk with one of my bosses about taking some time off, news would break somewhere else and I would be off on the road again. I complained to my friends about the burden, but the equal truth was that I was secretly relieved when news broke, because it diverted me from thinking about myself and my dilemma.

Getting sent to Northern Ireland was a welcome distraction. When I went back to Belfast, my birthplace, I was most concerned about avoiding my mother's indoctrination. Her identity as Ulster Protestant defines her to this day. Her home is full of Union Jacks and bulldogs and commemorative plates depicting the royal family. She hates the annual St. Patrick's Day parade in New York, especially the dyed green beer. When I was a child, on every St. Patrick's Day, she defiantly put orange ribbons in my hair while all the other children at school, whether Jewish, Italian, or Irish, wore green. I recited to anyone who would listen how a Protestant king had defeated a Catholic king three hundred years ago, and the Protestants need to wear orange in protest of this Irish Catholic holiday. I repeated the stories like a robot to the other girls at school, and I was so absorbed by my mother's prejudice that I actually felt contempt for the Catholic Irish-American children decked out in green and shamrocks. I felt betrayed if my close friends wore green on that day and didn't take my side and wear orange. It made no difference that she lived in New Jersey; my mother felt unseen. She felt nobody understood her identity in this Kennedy-worshiping country. So I grew up hearing only one side of that story. It wasn't her fault. People naturally tell their version of events. But it was another way that I learned about the roots of ethnic hatred in my own home.

When I went to Belfast as a reporter, I was easily accepted by Catholics and Protestants. Siobhan is a very common name in the Catholic community. Gerry Adams and his Sinn Fein party, the political wing of the IRA, welcomed me, assuming I was a sympathetic Irish-American Catholic. The Protestant Loyalists just needed to hear which street I was born on to assume I was one of theirs. The fact of the matter was that I was neither. I was some mixed-up half-Jew, half-Protestant who felt at home everywhere and nowhere and certainly didn't belong to any tribe. I can feel linked to another person through the shared human experience of tragedy or beauty or kindness but rarely along some superficial accident of shared geography. I'm more likely to feel kinship to a Bushman touched by the beauty of a sunset than a fellow Northern Irishman burning tires on Guy Fawkes Day.

Northern Ireland is one of those conflicts where the U.S. news media took a stand long ago and developed a knee-jerk sympathy for the IRA as the underdogs against British rule. I carefully monitored myself for any residual prejudice against the Catholic side from my childhood but I was also anxious to tell the less-heard Protestant viewpoint. As reporters we often cover the side that is most vocal, whoever plays the better victim. Sinn Fein were masters at getting their story out and fawned all over the press. The Protestants hadn't quite grasped that essential aspect of modern warfare: get the press on your side.

I was surprised to see the Orangemen in action. There was something archaic about these men who marched in bowler hats and sashes and went to bonfires burning the Irish tricolor and the pope in effigy. They were nothing like my mother. I was out covering a bonfire one night where just about everyone sported a tattoo and a beer can. I called my mother on my cell phone to describe the scene to her.

"I'm with your people," I told her.

"That crowd certainly aren't my people, I can assure you," said my mother in her haughtiest voice.

Sometimes I met people in Northern Ireland who could rise above their cultural and religious identities and find strength in their identity as humans—as fathers, as brothers, as people who simply wanted to live in peace. Usually something so terrible had happened to them that all those symbols of their identity had lost meaning, like a man I met the day after a cease-fire was declared by the IRA. His teenage daughter had been the last victim of sectarian violence—that round, anyway. She was a seventeen-year-old Catholic. She was shot dead in bed. Her crime? A Protestant boyfriend.

"I forgive her killers," her father told me and my crew, sitting in his garden two days after her death. "Revenge just keeps it going—you kill my child, I'll kill yours. Somebody has to stop the cycle. If my daughter's death stops this cycle, she won't have died in vain."

We stopped the camera. I thanked him, went into our van, and burst into tears. I have so many stored up for every mother I've interviewed who lost a son to an IRA bomb or every Balkan villager who has lost his home, and every husband who lost his wife in a plane crash. I have been collecting tears for so long that now the tiniest pinprick can unexpectedly unleash a torrent.

Then there are the ancient tears. They have waited a long time to wet my cheeks and come out of their dark well of hiding. The old ones mix with the new ones. A small girl's unshed tears. Tears so old and in need of shedding that any hint of sadness lures them to the surface.

It was during moments like these that I couldn't imagine ever doing anything else with my life. To witness people in their darkest moments reach inside themselves and find courage inspired me to do the same.

14

The "Swan" and the Land of Bunkers

When I sat down to think about the array of men I was dating in my thirties, I could finally see what any sensible person would have noticed right away: none of them wanted the same things I did. Trevor was an action junkie who was addicted to adrenaline, completely miswired for anything resembling a relationship; Julian was young and undomesticated, still looking at women as notches on his belt buckle. When Mel came along, talking about a burning desire to settle down and make babies, I thought he was the guy I had been waiting for.

OK, so he was forty and still lived with his mother in Beverly Hills, but that was because he came home when his father died and stayed a few years longer than expected. Sweet, I thought. This guy cares about family. Maybe I should have suspected something when I came to visit and we slept in his older sister's long-vacated room, frilly pink bedspread and all. I noted the parallel to my father and his unnatural attachment to his mother. But I could hardly write off every man simply because he had a mother. The other sign I underestimated was his constant worry about his weight. He was tall and skinny, but always stepping on and off the scales. Over the years I've learned to be wary of a man without a huge appetite. If they hold back at the dinner table, chances are they may show similar restraint in the bedroom.

There was something comforting in this tall, lumbering, matzo brei–eating Jewish male. He was smart and funny, and seemed to be just the type of person I should make a life with. Plus, he was a budding screenwriter, like everyone else in Los Angeles, so he could easily pack his computer and come to be with me wherever I had to go. I was smitten on our first date: dinner overlooking the Pacific Ocean in Los Angeles. Mel compared himself to a swan, wanting to mate for life. I was used to meeting men who were more apt to liken themselves to alpha-male baboons in search of a harem. I fell hard for it, responding with the story of a black swan I covered in England. When the swan's mate died, he seemed to be dying of loneliness himself, prompting a nationwide search to find him a new mate. Mel and I looked deeply into each other's eyes. It seemed right.

Then I started calculating. I was thirty-six. I had about a year more on my contract in London. If Mel and I could get to know each other transatlantically, when my contract came up we would be ready to settle down together. That way I could still have a couple of kids before I turned forty and have a reasonable engagement period before marriage. Like many other single women my age, I was getting obsessed with my biological clock. I had even reached the point where I was estimating the number of ovulations I had left in life.

"If I ovulate twelve times a year and I have eight more fertile years, that leaves only ninety-six chances to get pregnant!" I moaned to Francesca in a panic.

"There's always that doctor up in Scotland that cloned Dolly the sheep," Francesca offered.

"Yeah, maybe I can just clone myself, if worse comes to worst. At least I'd know what I was getting," I said.

It was more than an idle thought. I had just come back from reporting on Dolly, the famous first clone, who lived on a remote farm near Edinburgh. Meeting Dolly, a cuddly Fin Dorset lamb, was more exciting than the usual tin-pot dictator or guerrilla leader. As I put my hand in her pen and patted her woolly body, I felt I was reaching out and touching the next century. She had been made from a mammary cell of her so-called mother, hence the name Dolly, as in Dolly Parton. Dolly gave the media a chance to come up with all kinds of nightmare scenarios. Will we clone ourselves for spare parts? Will parents want backup children in case of damage or death? Will Saddam Hussein clone legions for an army? I had none of those concerns; instead, I thought of Dolly as a way out of depending on a man to fulfill my dream of motherhood.

Mel seemed right, and I daydreamed that my father had set us up from heaven. Maybe he had hooked up with Mel's recently deceased father to create a celestial shidech, Jewish matchmaking. I congratulated myself that I had waited for the right one to come along, someone who wanted the same things I did. And Uncle Leon would be so happy that I had found a Jewish guy. Mel was smart and funny and just neurotic enough to appreciate all my insecurities. He nicknamed me Cataclysmia, Melodramatica, Catastrophia, and Abandonia, making fun of my predilection to overdramatize any hint of trouble in our relationship.

Usually, whenever a friend or relative came to London to visit me, news would break and I would be sent off to cover some crisis.

I knew if Mel and I were to have a chance, I needed to be in London when he flew over to see me. I asked CNN not to send me anywhere for a month. In the preceding six weeks I had been in Moscow, Budapest, Belfast twice, and Edinburgh. My producers in Atlanta were understanding and said I could stay and cover London stories and let some of the other correspondents do the traveling.

Sure enough, the day after Mel arrived there was a midair plane crash in India. The producer who called pretended to feel bad for a moment, but then got back to business, insisting that there was nobody else who was available. Always the good soldier, I agreed to go. It didn't matter that my boyfriend had just flown halfway around the world to see me; I didn't have the guts to say no to CNN. Leaving Mel and Max alone in my apartment, I got on the next plane.

After landing in New Delhi, I drove four hours through the night to the chickpea and mustard fields where a Saudi Airways aircraft and Kazakh Air cargo plane had collided. Falling from the sky at twenty thousand feet does terrible things to a body. It bloats heads and torsos so they look like swollen caricatures. The makeshift mortuary set up at a nearby school presented a whole new experience of death. The bodies were brought in, lain out gently, and draped in white muslin as smoke swirled about the rooms from the Hindu prayer fires. The burning incense scented the air sweetly with sandalwood but couldn't quite mask the intolerable, putrid stench of human death. Bodies waiting for identification were carefully lined up, like empty vessels, no longer able to carry the spirits that once inhabited them. Family members came to identify them, but there was none of the Balkan or Caucasian wailing at the side of a loved one. Instead, I saw a resigned acceptance of transmuting spirits. Perhaps in a society where life is viewed as transitory, there is greater peace with death. I did a couple of stories on the crash, as well as one on the treacherous air-traffic control conditions at the New Delhi airport. The experience did nothing for my already considerable anxiety about flying, but like so many things, I tried to keep it from my mind. I got back to London just in time for Mel to leave. He tried to be understanding, but this was no way to have a relationship.

I knew I had to make time for Mel if it was ever going to work. But sure enough, the next time we planned a visit, I was shipped off to Albania. Perhaps I should have been thinking about my relationship; instead I became engrossed in another news assignment. It was a rare chance to go to a country that had always intrigued me. Albania was the most secretive and backward of all the former Communist states. After five decades of Stalinist repression, it was considered one of the world's most isolated countries. It was also Europe's poorest country. Enver Hoxha, who had ruled Albania for decades, was so paranoid he broke off ties with the Soviets and Chinese for straying too far from Stalinist ideals. After years of deprivation and poverty, cut off from the rest of the world and told they lived in paradise, Albanians were shocked when the old regime fell and television from the rest of Europe was suddenly available. It showed them a world of luxury and decadence that they didn't even know existed. In a land with few cars, where people still depended on horse-drawn carts, where rock and roll, jeans, and even beards had been banned as symbols of Western capitalism, Albania made the former Soviet Union look like southern California.

Now Albania was making the transition to democracy, but the country's desperate poverty paved the way for trouble. Albanians were easy targets for get-rich-quick cons. Pyramid schemes flourished. Then one huge pyramid swept the country and collapsed suddenly, taking many people's savings with it. Albanians started rioting and the country descended into a shooting gallery as angry citizens broke into weapons-storage facilities and started firing stolen guns indiscriminately in the streets. After decades of strict law and order, a taste of freedom brought on dizzying chaos. It was as if a nation of children had been let out of school and was having a giant temper tantrum. Schoolteachers, artists, waiters, and businessmen all took part in a frenzy of stealing and looting. It was not so much a murderous rampage as a way of rebelling, letting off steam.

In his paranoia, Hoxha had built 700,000 bunkers across this tiny country to ward off attack from the United States, the Chinese, and the Soviets. They were concrete pillboxes big enough for a man and his gun, an indestructible reminder of the impoverished country's insular mind-set. Almost every visible piece of open landscape was bunkerized. Now, after the collapse of the old order, they stood like poisoned toadstools, blighting a beautiful Adriatic country and condemning its people to a mentality of distrust and fear of the outside, rendering them badly unprepared for the enemy that had erupted from within. I was fascinated by the bunkers; they were both tragic and humorous. Some Albanians grasped the irony, and sold small alabaster bunkers as tourist souvenirs. I bought as many as I could carry, and to this day I have eight dotting my living room. Whenever we were out shooting our story of the day, I'd insist on stopping to film one more bunker. They were always stuck in some incongruous place, in a schoolyard, a vineyard, the beaches, farms, front yards. They even watched over the dead in the cemeteries. I did almost two dozen stories out of Albania about the looting, shooting, and embassy evacuations, but it was the piece I did on the bunkers, those useless bulwarks against invasion from the outside, that told Albania's real story.

Besides the bunkers, there was the relentless sound of gunfire. Armed with ransacked weapons and unlimited ammunition, Albanians fired their guns day and night. Usually they weren't firing at anyone, just randomly into the air. The noise didn't stop for weeks. I couldn't hear birds chirping. I couldn't hear car horns sounding. I just heard gunfire twenty-four hours a day. I heard it when I woke up in the morning and when I went to sleep at night. I sometimes wondered if a stray bullet might come through my window, but I'd quickly put that thought away and cover my head with a pillow, as if it might offer some protection.

As with everything, I got used to it quickly. The gunfire was so loud, my mother could hardly hear me over the phone line when I called to tell her my visit home with Mel had been delayed.

"Is everything OK?" she asked tentatively, never making a big deal about the dangers of my job.

"Oh, yes, they are just shooting into the air, not at us." I wanted to alleviate her anxiety but I also wanted to bask in it for a moment. I was not used to hearing her worry about me.

"Yes, but whatever goes up has to come down somewhere."

She had a point. I thought we should be walking around wearing helmets but nobody else was, and I would have been embarrassed to overtly show fear. She changed the subject. "How are the carpets? I bet they have fine ceramics," my mother inquired, making sure I didn't miss a shopping opportunity wherever I was.

The situation deteriorated so much that eventually all the foreign embassies decided to evacuate their staffs. U.S. helicopter pilots were reluctant to fly in at first, deterred by the constant gunfire. The Italians, who had more experience on the ground in Albania, were the first to start ferrying out embassy dependents. Once the marines saw, via CNN, that the Italians were braving the random fire to bring out people, they sent choppers into the U.S. embassy compound.

At the same time that Albanians were marauding in the streets with their pilfered arms, and the marines were ferrying foreigners out to safety, President Bill Clinton pulled a muscle in his leg. Producers in Atlanta, who had been briefly interested in this country they had never heard of because there were lots of guns going off, instantly lost interest. But as usual, my producers wanted me to stay on indefinitely.

Making sense of a country stuck in the fifteenth century, like reporting on a sheep from the twenty-first century, was all in a day's work. But finding a way to share my bizarre world with a man was proving impossible. I had expected to be in Albania for five or six days, but I was there for three weeks. Mel went home.

In principle, Mel liked the idea of a tough modern woman hanging around wars, but not the reality of flying across the ocean to see me, then for me to disappear. I couldn't blame him. He had good intentions and really thought he wanted an accomplished woman who could match his intellect and ambition. But when it came down to it, he really seemed just to want someone like his mother: a polished, well-educated woman who stayed at home and devoted herself to taking care of him. Maybe I should have known when he said, "My mother is a huge part of my life. Anyone who loves me has to accept that." What that meant, I found, was that everything, including me, came second to his mother. But I suppose in my turn I was saying everything came second to CNN.

After six months of traveling back and forth, talking with me via phone and e-mail, Mel announced that he was "confused," a code word I recognized in modern lingo that means "I want out." I wondered whether it had anything to do with meeting my family. We had just had a visit to Highland Park, New Jersey, where Mel got a full dose of the eccentricities of my tribe. There was the usual gathering of strays that my mother collects, ranging from a visiting Chinese professor who barely spoke English to her "park friends," the assorted dog fanatics that my mother picks up at the park when out walking her beloved charges. She always finds some needy and often strange human to invite over.

Uncle Leon may have pushed him over the edge. He was so excited to see this big Jewish guy with a great education that he couldn't stop himself from interrogating Mel on his intentions. "So, Mel, are you thinking of marriage? You know I never married and I regret it every day of my life. A man is nothing without a wife and family, nothing. When I see a nice young man like you I hate to think you'll end up alone," Uncle Leon lectured, employing his usual subtlety. "You know Siobhan has a college degree from Duke University." I was waiting to see if he'd mention the fact that I have no cavities. He often urges me in his weekly letters to get my teeth cleaned. Sure enough, that was next.

"Doesn't Siobhan have a great smile? A man doesn't want a woman with missing teeth, and all the Darrow girls have good teeth. My father was a dentist, so we understand the importance of good teeth." Mel looked aghast.

Maybe the potential gene pool frightened Mel off. I was disappointed that he didn't appreciate the charm and quirkiness of the characters he met, but I couldn't really blame him for leaving. Few men would put up with my erratic schedule and lifestyle. I thought Uncle Leon would be heartbroken that Mel and I were finished, but he was philosophical, sending me his own brand of wisdom when he heard the news.

Dear Siobhan,

I believe you made the right decision in ending the relationship with Mel. The fact that a man still lives with his mother at his age and has never been married should raise a red flag that there is a serious drawback in his makeup and that he is probably not husband material.

A case in point is myself. I had joined a singles club and had quite a few dates. The minute I uttered a discordant remark such as, What do you think of the AIDS epidemic, I realized I doomed the relationship right then and there. In another instance, as soon as a prospective date heard that I didn't have a car to pick her up with, she dropped me right then and there. We live in a very self-serving world.

Affectionately,
Uncle Leon

I knew I should figure out what was going wrong every time I had and then lost a man. But I didn't allow myself much time to mope about Mel. Soon after, the U.S. and British television-viewing public became transfixed by the trial of Louise Woodward, the English nanny who was convicted of causing the death of the baby left in her charge. I was dispatched to her hometown, Elton, in northern England. Mandy, a producer from South Africa, Todd, the cameraman, and I made the five-hour trip north and arrived at the Rigger Pub, which was to be our home for the next five days. I was chained to a live satellite truck and on air day and night feeding the network's huge appetite for this tabloid-turned-news story. Louise Woodward's hometown had set up a "Free Louise Woodward" committee and was operating out of the local pub. I was surrounded by chain-smoking, drunken Brits recently in touch with their inner child. It was so packed inside the pub that they were either spilling beer on me or weeping all over me. I started wondering if my mother had been right that the British had been better before Diana's death unleashed their long-pent-up emotions. Rupert Murdoch's Sky Television installed a giant TV screen in the pub so the locals could watch the trial live. Every time the camera would cut to the pub, the crowd cheered and chanted, "Free Louise!"

After eighteen-hour days crammed in the pub reporting on the outpouring of support for this hometown girl and inhaling so much cigarette smoke I felt like suing CNN for secondhand-smoke damage, we headed out in search of food before collapsing for a few hours back at our hotel. One night all we could find was Kentucky Fried Chicken. We all sat huddled in our van at eleven-thirty at night ravenously gnawing on Colonel Sanders's finest, and I had a moment of déjà vu.

A year before I had been sitting hunched on a bench with my crew in Magnitogorsk, a town in the Urals where the sky is black from the steel mills. We were covering the Russian elections from the hinterlands. We were eating Cup-a-Soup for dinner outside in the cold because inside in our hotel the stench of urine was so strong, it killed the appetite. Todd had been the cameraman on that trip too.

"I can't believe instead of having a real dinner with my husband and kids, I'm eating this slop in the middle of nowhere with you guys. Nothing personal," I said to Todd.

"Think of us as your family," said Todd in an effort to soothe.

Todd was right: my colleagues were like a surrogate family, and I knew many of them almost as well as I would a spouse. I always knew to order Todd a Coke when we stopped for food. I could read his moods; I knew his habits; I knew that he knew every word to every Beatles song and that I could count on him to take the most compelling pictures in any event we covered.

The Louise Woodward story became a lightning rod for all the fears of working mothers who leave their kids with au pairs and nannies. It shocked Americans into paying more attention to who was raising their children. For me, it was one more big reminder that I was thirty-seven, alone, and had no babies of my own. I realized I was so worn out that if I didn't start taking care of myself, I would never be in any condition to have them. The bureau was understaffed in London, so I ran from one country to the next without a break in between. I would be in Moscow for a couple of weeks, then be shipped off to the Middle East with maybe a two-hour stopover at Heathrow airport. The London bureau manager, Ros Jackman, was heroic in her efforts to make our hectic lives easier. She would get some warm-weather clothes from my flat sent out to the airport. She helped me arrange elaborate Max transfers: he would head off to a dog-sitter alone in a minicab every time I jetted off to cover another disaster.

A few weeks later, Prince Charles had given complementary medicine a big plug in a speech. I was sent out to do a story, so we hunted down a clinic that specialized in faith healing and other nontraditional remedies. My interviewee, a high-tech homeopathic practitioner, used a computer to analyze her patient's electrophysiological reactivity to determine the condition of his or her organs. She wired me up to her contraption by using Velcro straps around my head, wrists, and ankles to show me how it worked. After a few moments, with raised eyebrows, she issued a stern warning: "Your exhaustion level is off the monitor and your adrenal glands are stuck in the on position, putting constant pressure on all your organs. You need to give your adrenal glands a break and take a long rest or you could get seriously ill."

I don't know if her fancy computer figured all that out or she had just taken one look at me and my haggard face and the bags under my eyes, but what she said rang true. She gave me some drops to turn off my adrenal gland for a while. I went back to the bureau and wrote my story and then went home and decided I was going to turn off my adrenal glands for good. I was constantly sick, which I blamed on drizzly British weather, but now I thought that maybe my body was screaming for attention in the only way it knew how. I realized I was not indestructible and I had to stop living like this. I had to stop running and being wrenched from my home and any semblance of routine. My life felt so out of control that I just wanted to hide under my desk when any story broke. I hadn't picked up my dry cleaning in weeks. I hadn't been to a grocery store. I knew the configuration of furniture in Heathrow's business-class lounge better than in my own living room. Every time I set foot in the airport, I would frantically dial my sisters or Lori or whatever man I was with at the time, desperate for a lifeline, a moment of connection to a saner world before being hurled into the epicenter of another news story. I was running so fast that my life just felt like a blur.

I had one of the most coveted jobs in television news, as London correspondent for CNN, with a front-row seat to every major history-making event, but I had to walk away. I had collected so much input from the outside world, it was time to turn inward and see what I had amassed. I needed to rummage around all those half-forgotten treasures of experience, one heaped atop the next, like a closetful of exquisite designer clothes that were never worn. I needed to stop and listen to myself, that person I had been running from and for whom I seemed to have had no time. I wanted to get comfortable inside and wear my self like a long-lost sweater I used to love but had left neglected in the bottom of a drawer for so long I had forgotten I had it. It was no longer all about trying to find a man to save me; I needed to save myself.

Spinning

I knew I was really in California when my yoga instructor told the class to mentally thank the room for being there. That came after a lengthy explanation of why we should spend ten minutes a day inverted, meaning standing on our heads. Creatures that spend time upside down every day, like bats, escape arthritis and suffer less stress than those mammals that haven't discovered the benefits of a change of perspective, the teacher said.

I had just turned my whole life upside down. I told my bosses at CNN that I needed some time off, and I moved to California. I packed up my Central Asian carpets, my socialist realist paintings, my Russian antiques, and even my minishrine to the world's dictators, including my Saddam Hussein engraved platter and old Stalinist propaganda posters, and, with Max, headed to Santa Monica.

My first real encounter with the natives was a "spin" class: a roomful of beautiful people pumping away at stationary bikes, with a teacher distracting us from the physical pain with loud music and inspirational life commentary. Greville, an English refugee who had broken free of any bonds of reserve with which he was brought up, was my favorite teacher. He reminded us to drink water while exercising—"you need to hydrate like the flowers in your garden." During another spin class, Greville put on Strauss to cycle by and asked if anyone had lived a past life in Vienna. This was a perfectly normal question in Los Angeles. I knew I was going to like it here. After years of neglecting my physical and mental health, it felt good to be in a place where people went overboard in the other direction. When I moved into my new condo, the barefoot landscaper told me it was an auspicious day to move in, in lunar terms, and gave me some sage to burn. Nobody would think me odd here for my occasional visits to a clairvoyant. Even the *Los Angeles Times* has a daily astrological forecast and, in my new life, it was often the only part of the paper I read.

I relished going to sleep in the same bed every night and waking up there with no plane to catch and no story to cover. I woke up each morning with a long, sun-soaked day stretching out before me, and nothing to do. After all those years of deadlines and time pressure caused by events I could not control, facing an eternity of time with nothing hanging over my head was luxurious, a feeling I hadn't encountered since childhood summer breaks from school. I could meander into my own feelings and thoughts without limits. I spent time cooking, which I had almost forgotten how to do for years. I slept a lot. Sometimes I took two naps a day. My exhaustion was so deep that the naps always felt as if they were just chipping away at a mountain of sleep deprivation stored inside me. I started feeling muscles relax that I didn't even know had been tensed for years. My shoulders seemed to drop a few inches.

Of course, sometimes that expanse of time seemed ominous. I

had a tinge of fear that I wouldn't find something meaningful to fill the time. Mostly, though, it felt like wide-open sky or like looking out to the ocean. Memories wafted up from deep inside me that I hadn't thought of in years. I wrote them down, capturing them quickly before they drifted back into the dark for another decade.

Sometimes my old reality intruded. When air strikes hit Baghdad in December 1998, I watched from the comfort of my sofa with Max curled at my side. It was amazing to see what entertainment war appeared to be from this end of the camera. I sat with my dinner in front of the TV, tuning in to the surgical strikes. I noticed all the hype and drumroll that CNN used to rev up viewers before they cut live to Baghdad. To me, it felt like the ultimate in voyeurism, like craning your neck to see a car wreck. There was a vicarious thrill of danger and clearly defined good guys and bad guys, and it made great entertainment. During all those years that I had been visiting battlefields to get the "news," I had had little idea of how it actually came across on TV as entertainment, competing with reruns of *N.Y.P.D. Blue*. When I got tired of watching, I could just switch the channel and watch *Ally McBeal* or read a book or take Max for a walk, just like everyone else.

But a few months later when Kosovo flared up, something drew me back in. I watched NATO planes send wave after wave of missile attacks on the Serbs. Only this time I couldn't turn off the TV. I found myself crying as I watched. I couldn't stop crying. I cried for all the times I had gone into villages and interviewed refugees crammed twenty or thirty into a room. I felt a powerful urge to go there, wanting to help tell their story to the world. I felt guilty sitting on my sofa, immobilized, not doing anything.

I was enraged by the U.S. coverage of the war, which demonized the Serbs in an oversimplistic way, mindlessly repeating NATO jargon about morality. I wanted to yell, "It doesn't matter who is right and who is wrong; people are suffering!" I wanted a chance to get in front of the cameras again, to describe the trauma of Albanian refugees crossing the mountains, cold and afraid, after being driven from their homes. Or to talk about the Serb in a black woolen mask who had knocked on the door and ordered the Albanians out, pained beneath his surface anger. I could explain that he hadn't been born bad, that I might have even been to the village his family was driven from, where his grandmother probably died in a concentration camp run by Croatian fascists and he had been weaned on stories about the cruel Croats and Albanians.

I knew I couldn't go back there. My time had passed. And yet I felt so drawn to it because it had been my life for so long, covering breaking news like that, and pitching in with CNN in a crisis. As I watched with tears streaming down my face, I thought, I might as well be there, because I can't turn off the TV. I was mesmerized, trapped by the feelings of images stirred up in me, the fear, the sense of futility, of feeling like a coward to sit and weep and not do anything.

I picked up the phone to call CNN, to volunteer to go. Then panic gripped my neck. I didn't want to go. I didn't want to leave my sofa. I didn't want to see any more. I turned off the TV.

I was like a junkie for whom the only thing that will make her better is the very thing that hurts her most. There I was, frozen on the couch with the phone in one hand, feeling so terrible and repelled by what I saw, yet so drawn to the violence and the crisis. The only thing that would break my paralysis, I thought, would be to go. I dialed the number but hung up before anyone answered. This isn't my war, I thought. I need to fight my own battle. I'm like an alcoholic on the wagon about to take a drink; I can't go there again.

I remembered a house I had visited once with my camera crew. It almost doesn't matter where it was because I have been to that house so many times in so many villages. We pulled up and knocked on the door. We had driven past a stream of people, some of them on foot lugging hastily packed suitcases, others piled onto tractors with their clothes, a few pots and pans and family photos stuffed into sheets. Families uprooted in moments, trudging through mud and snow and not sure where they were going. They walked slowly, their eyes blank with fear. The children held on tightly to their parents' hands. The door opened to a crowded one-room house. Twenty people were now living in a place hardly big enough for two, sharing one bathroom and sleeping huddled on the floor. It was the home of a farmer, and I marveled at his humanity. I saw sadness and generosity in the eyes of this man, who took in fifteen of the tired arrivals, his wife baking flatbread to feed the hungry strangers. I interviewed a scared young mother who didn't know where her husband was. She didn't know how she would feed her children or where they would go next. She said she hoped to go home soon. But I knew better. I had seen her so many times before in so many places. I had just come from her village and I had seen what the soldiers were doing there. Maybe that had been her house burning. The true extent of what she had just endured might take years to absorb. She might no longer have a home to go back to. I had also seen her husband many times. He was no longer the farmer who got up before sunrise to work the fields to feed her and her children. Now he hid in the hills with the other men and used his rifle to take aim at his enemy. She might never see him again. I was touched by this mother, who thought to grab her son's teddy bear as they ran from their home. But I knew it wouldn't be enough to comfort the boy or make him ever forget what happened. He would grow up hating, and yearning to return home with vengeance in his heart. It was unbearable, this misery and cruelty and terror I saw. For only now could I see it. Only now, while watching it on TV thousands of miles away. I was safe in my home and I felt their helplessness. I knew what it was like to be small and scared.

I knew I couldn't go back into war zones. My armor was no longer in place and I had no more stomach for war, which always seemed to be about the same thing. Nobody ever wins. It never works. Whether an army is defeated or victorious, the wounds to the soul are the same.

Finally the war passed. I was able to resume my rehabilitation. In the evenings I watched sitcoms to reconnect with my countrymen. How could I live here and converse meaningfully with the natives if I'd never seen an episode of *Seinfeld?* Other simple things had great meaning to me, like being able to take time to shop around for car and health insurance instead of frantically choosing the first one I could find. Cleaning up my internal and external world went hand in hand. I threw out clothes, shoes, and books I had been lugging around forever.

A few weeks after I moved into my new place, I went into the closet to look for something. I noticed a cardboard box. It was taped shut, still unopened from my transatlantic move. I must have glanced at it dozens of times, but this time something made me want to open it. It was full of musty letters. I pulled everything out of the box and let myself drift into the past. There were stacks of letters from my college boyfriend Michael, my grades from Duke University, and letters from my college roommate Karen while I was doing a semester in Moscow. There were letters from men all over the world: an expatriate living in Tokyo who seemed to have exiled himself to Japan much as I had to Russia, an Italian whom I met on a plane en route to London—soulful, imploring letters from men I could barely remember, from would-be suitors whom I had kept at arm's length. Overlapping loves, none of whom I really gave myself to.

I read them all, scanning each letter for scraps, evidence about who I was, scouring each line for another clue about myself. If I kept reading, I thought, maybe I'd come into focus. Who was this girl who ran away to Russia at twenty, who decided to throw her lot in with a country considered the enemy by her homeland, who felt so ill at ease in her own skin that only by going to what felt like another planet could she temporarily dull her discomfort?

I reread the yellowed newspaper clippings about the divided-spouse cases like mine. They described the tragedy of Americans married to Soviets who were barred from leaving the country. It read like ancient history. It made me feel like a fraud. I wondered if I was ever really in that marriage. I liked the high drama of two superpowers being involved in my life; it made me feel fleetingly important, but it didn't seem real. Who was I? A cruel and careless lover, as described in some of Michael's letters, or the passionate, warm, rare woman he wrote about in others? Was I the wise, philo-sophical friend my roommate wrote of, always at peace and self-assured on a journey of discovery to Russia? Or was I a troubled girl running as far away as possible from a family torn apart by cancer and bitterness? Was I running away from my pain or was I chasing adventure? I looked through the dusty, handwritten, scribbled lines for evidence of me. I stared hard at the photos of this girl sitting alone on the Great Wall of China, shivering in the snow in Red Square, and floating in the Dead Sea.

I was a girl who had used the chaotic and painful experiences from her own home to understand an enemy nation eight thousand miles away. I was a woman in the middle of her own personal strug-gle who still got through college and built a foundation for an extraordinary life. I was a woman who, no matter how many relationships she botched up, still had enough hope to try again. I was the cruel girlfriend and the loving and compassionate one. I was wise and philosophical, and I was a lost soul. I was merely human.

I couldn't repack the box. I left the letters and photos scattered on the table. Let them breathe for a while, I thought. Let these old wounds get some air. To heal.

16

Dunkin' Donuts

When I was fifteen, I got a job at Dunkin' Donuts. I served coffee to the local police force and assorted strays who would hang out at the Formica counter. I was a flirtatious teenager with attitude. I loved all the attention that my short pink-and-white uniform helped attract, even if it was just from a bunch of cops and construction workers.

My best friends at work were Lois and her mother, Lorraine. They had been working behind that counter for years, first to help Lois's son through college, and then to get him through law school. Lois was in her forties, although a hard life and lots of cigarettes seemed to have added a decade to her face. Lorraine was in her sixties and could have passed for eighty. They were tough, chainsmoking women who cussed and swore and acted as though they had little use for anyone, especially anyone male. But they were endlessly kind and mothering to me. Lorraine, her face hardly visible under a large colony of warts, barked and snarled at the customers as she shuffled up and down the counter, dragging her lame foot. They were terrified of her, but she always spoke gently to me. Sometimes Lois would work double shifts because Lorraine wasn't well. The sight of Lois's nicotine-stained fingers tugged at me. I knew her pack of Kool cigarettes helped keep her awake through the overnight shift covering for Lorraine, but I worried about her health.

I loved the job. I gave great service, usually with a large dose of sarcasm. If anyone bugged me, anything might end up in their coffee. Lorraine and Lois had taught me how to handle the public. I loved the paycheck too, and it usually disappeared fast at the mall, where I went with my girlfriends to buy jeans, halter tops, and purple mascara, the kind of necessities that adolescent girls craved in the seventies. I looked forward to my afternoon shifts at Dunkin' Donuts. Above all, it was a way to get out of my house. My father was dying of cancer and my parents spent so much energy fighting each other that there seemed to be little left to battle the disease. It wasn't talked about. Confusion, instability, and pain hung silently in the air, and I could feel it permeating my body whenever I walked through our front door. The bank was in the process of foreclosing on our house, giving some solidity to the amorphous sense of doom. Dunkin' Donuts felt like a refuge.

I remember staring out the window, imagining myself coming back someday to this small town as a big celebrity, pulling up into the Dunkin' Donuts parking lot in a fancy car and being somebody famous instead of the girl behind the counter pouring coffee.

One day while I was at work after school, a cute guy came in. He wasn't some loser, like the usual blue-collar type I flirted with casually. He had long hair, looked earthy, and was in his thirties. He drove a van. We talked about what I was reading in my high school honors English class as he had a glazed doughnut and a cup of decaf. He started coming by occasionally. I started watching for his van to pull into the parking lot.

One day he asked if I wanted to go for a drive with him after work. I was thrilled at the invitation. I could not believe such a cool older guy would have any interest in me. Even Lois, who didn't trust any male, thought he seemed a step above the usual clientele. I punched my card in the time clock, put a sweater over my waitress uniform, and hopped into his van with him. We drove awhile and talked. I felt grown-up just being in a guy's car. He headed to the woods near the university and asked if I smoked dope. "Sure, I've been smoking since my freshman year," I said. He drove to the middle of nowhere and stopped the van.

"Let's go back here and have a beer," he said, steering me toward the back of the van where there was a small table and a bed.

"Do you live in here?" I asked.

He didn't answer; instead he started kissing me and touching my breasts through my pink uniform. I was surprised and a little nervous, but I liked the attention. I didn't stop him.

He unzipped my dress and pulled it up over my head. I started getting scared. Before I knew what was happening, he was pulling down my underpants. I didn't know what to do so I lay there, paralyzed, holding my breath.

I felt something hard and strange pushing at me, something alien. I had never even seen a penis before, having had only sisters. The texture of his pubic hair against my thigh frightened me. It came as a shock to me that a penis even came with pubic hair.

"What are you doing?" I asked him, trying to pull away.

"I'm balling you."

I was more offended somehow by the choice of word—it seemed so crude and unromantic—than by the fact that I felt I couldn't say no. We were far from anyone. I didn't believe I could stop him. I had willingly gone with him. I had allowed him to touch me. I was afraid to make him mad. I closed my eyes and went away, somewhere deep inside where nobody could hurt me, and let him do it to me. I didn't feel anything. I didn't know how to stand up for myself. I had never known my feelings mattered. I told myself it didn't matter. I wasn't there anymore.

He never came into Dunkin' Donuts again. Lois asked me once whatever happened to the nice guy who used to hang around. "He seemed to like you so much," she said. It left me deeply confused, though I was so young at the time I didn't even understand my own confusion. I even wondered, with some hope, if he might want to be my boyfriend. But I never saw him again. I was ashamed to tell her I had somehow managed to frighten him away. I was too embarrassed to tell her or anyone else about what happened. So I said nothing. It took almost fifteen more years and more men I didn't know how to say no to before I realized my first sexual encounter had been a rape.

One afternoon many years later, when I was in my late twenties, Lori and I were recounting our sexual escapades to each other. I told her that I had often felt as though I was not a willing participant in sex. It was always something I thought I had to do to earn love. I told her about that day in Dunkin' Donuts. I hadn't thought about it in a long time, and it was only as I started telling her that I understood the weight of what I was saying.

It took another decade to understand that the place I had disappeared to that day in the woods was the same place I went whenever I was sent to a war zone as a correspondent. And I came to realize that it still happens; it is where I go when anyone gets too close to me. I disappear into that numb place where I can be safe and untouched. A very old part of me resides in that place, hunkered down and buttressed by defenses. Locked away, this part of me taunts and torments, casting stones in the shadows of my mind. In the light, it gives me knowledge and strength. It is as though there is another person who emerges from that place. She is my original, true self. She went into hiding for a few decades because her first experiences with the world were frightening. But it feels safe to come out now.

17

The Blind Date

When I arrived in California, at thirty-eight years old, I called everyone I knew and told them I was interviewing husbands. Lori offered her usual practical advice: "You need to treat this like a job," she said. "Use all your sources. Be a reporter. Research their pasts. Be methodical. Slash and burn."

I had a profile in my mind of the kind of man I wanted to meet: a Rhodes scholar, well-off, worldly, gorgeous, and a hunk, with a great sense of humor and lots of heart, and no ex-wives, children, or mother. But my screening process was still faulty enough that I'd also consider the guy pouring coffee at Starbucks. Anyone who showed any interest tapped into my hunger for love. It was a hunger that I was beginning to nourish on my own. Now that I was spending much of my days writing, the memories I retrieved and wrote about were my new companions as I walked the beach with

Max. But the quiet let me realize how much I wanted a human companion as well.

Friends introduced me to all types. I met a few on my own. I figured that regular dating would be a whole new experience compared with the madness of meeting men on the road. Things could go forward at a more normal pace. It didn't have to happen all at once. I knew I would be in the same place the next week and even the next month. I could get to know someone in real time, instead of just meeting once or twice, then filling in the rest with my own fantasy. I could be more discerning. I had time to breathe in all the love I had in my life. I had my sisters, my friends, and Max. I finally felt comfortable with myself.

I had assumed that when I quit working, ready to stay still and make room for a man in my life, that he would suddenly, magically appear. I felt so ready—ready to sip coffee together on Sunday morning, to go food shopping as a pair, all that normal kind of stuff. Of course, that's not the way it happened. Lots of men showed up, but none of them was quite right. Was I just being too fussy? Or not fussy enough? Anyone who showed even remote interest, I considered, although the real possibilities I found a way to discredit.

"No more blind dates," I announced to Francesca during one of our morning marathon conversations.

"What was wrong with this one?"

"He had to get permission from his parole officer to take me out."

"Child molester?" asked Francesca, with characteristic nonchalance.

"No, fraud." This guy was a gambling addict who had stolen, cheated, and lied to feed his habit. Bad checks, embezzling, stealing from his girlfriend. He had gotten out of jail six weeks previously. I was his first date in three years.

"Poor thing," said Francesca. She has a soft spot for losers.

Not that he didn't make an interesting dinner companion. As usual, when in an uncomfortable situation, I shifted into reporter mode and questioned him closely about what life was like in prison, how the food was, all the while keeping a close eye on my handbag.

"Am I asking for too much?" I asked Francesca. I wanted someone who could make me laugh, who could earn a decent living, who wanted to make love with me, and whom I couldn't keep my hands off. And who didn't have a prison record. Why was this so hard?

"It only takes one," Francesca counseled. "You haven't been really looking that long. Be patient; the right one will come along."

Easy for her to say, I thought, living in her comfortable world with her new baby and devoted husband. When Hadi was dying, Francesca met a man at work. He came up to her in the hallway at the bank where they worked and asked if she would have dinner with him. She looked at him as if he were insane. "I barely get home to bathe," she told him. "I go right from work to the hospital every day, where my boyfriend is dying of cancer, and then I get home at eleven every night to feed my cat and fall into bed to get up and get here to work. No, I don't think I can have dinner with you." She walked off after her tirade, thinking that must have been the most dramatic rejection that that guy ever got.

The next day she apologized for being so abrupt. He smiled. His name was David. They became friends. David could tell she wasn't eating, and made her food and brought it in to work. He kept a respectful distance, but took care of her the best he could. After Hadi died, David asked Francesca out again.

A year later they were married and expecting a baby. David was completely different from the men Francesca had been out with in the past. He was a redhead with freckles, not the swarthy, Middle Eastern type she usually went for. He was all-American. He wanted the same things she did: a life partner, a baby, a dog.

After returning to America, I started speaking to Francesca twice a day on the phone. I told her about every date I went on, recounting the dialogue, analyzing each one in excruciating detail, and assessing each man's potential as a husband. In return, I heard about her baby's every new facial expression or utterance. We never tired of the minutiae of each other's lives. I didn't care how many times she told me she was fat; I always told her I was fatter. I must have asked her a thousand times if I'd end up alone; she always reassured me that I wouldn't.

While Francesca listened endlessly to my dating sagas, my older sister, Alexandra, was more pragmatic. Instead of listening to me whine, she hunted around for suitable men for me, sizing up fellow lawyers and scouring her husband's architectural firm for any interesting, unattached men. When I visited her and her family in Chicago, some stray male would often appear casually, but despite her best intentions, nothing ever took.

I eventually met my cybersurgeon, Larry, in the flesh. He was in the midst of a messy divorce. He was almost perfect-looking, and, I quickly realized, too perfect for my taste. Nips and tucks had rendered him younger-looking than I, even though he was ten years older. And he was way too nice to feel real. But "nice" was not applicable to his eighty-one-year-old Jewish mother. I met her at a party at his house. I said to her that it was strange how so many people looked alike at the party, and she said many of the guests were products of her son's handiwork.

"My son does the best nose in town," she announced proudly, pointing across the room at some peaked-looking creature who looked as though she hadn't had a meal in weeks. "He fixed half the noses here."

Once I let her know gently that her son was not the man for me, she gave me the rundown on all the bachelors at the party. She might have been surprised that anyone could pass Larry up, but I'm sure she was relieved that a half-breed like me wasn't going to steal away her nice Jewish doctor of a son.

"That one is a dentist, cute, and nice as can be, but you should have seen him before Larry worked on him," she whispered after pointing out a man across the room.

"God knows what the kids might look like," I whispered back.

She nodded conspiratorially. She had free time on her hands, and knew all the doctors in Beverly Hills, so I figured I should put her to work. Plus she knew the before and after, important information in a town where you can never be sure what you are getting, genetically speaking. Once they've had their nose jobs, eye tucks, face-lifts, and laser peels, the original is completely transformed. I did go out a few times with the cybersurgeon, but ultimately I was too busy overhauling my interior to understand his world of exteriors. He was fine for cyberspace, but I wanted the real thing.

18

Sperm Bank and Beyond

On my endless stream of blind dates, I felt like I was just wading through leftovers or defective models. I wondered whether Francesca was right when she said that all the good ones were taken by the time they reached thirty. I still felt pangs of hope and excitement when a friend mentioned that they wanted to introduce me to someone, imagining that this time it would be different, that as soon as I opened the door to him I would feel it, see something in his eyes, in the way he smelled, musky and male. I'd want to brush against him to catch a better whiff. I wouldn't even remember our conversation, it would flow so easily, but mostly I'd be wishing he would just touch my hand, and when he did I'd picture us in bed together. And later we'd make love for hours and then light candles and soak in my bathtub, and before I knew it, it would be dawn. And waking up to him padding around my apartment would feel as though he had always been there. And then I really opened the door and felt the inevitable disappointment. A friend suggested I stop looking for a man, and wait for him to find me.

The problem with waiting was that I wanted a baby. In magazines and newspapers I often read about actresses or other celebrities who gave birth into their late forties, so I had managed to block out a sense of urgency. Then I met a woman who told me she decided to have a baby at age thirty-eight, and was told by her doctor that she could not. When I looked into it, I discovered that a woman's chances of being able to give birth to a child naturally starts to diminish sharply at age thirty-eight, and that after forty her fertile years might as well be counted in canine years.

It was a shock, a real wake-up call. Suddenly I felt compelled to consider having a baby on my own. It seemed like a drastic step. I replayed my recent blind dates in my mind. Would hooking up with any of those men be preferable to being a single mother? The unfortunate answer was: No. Maybe I was just destined to be alone. Or maybe I would meet someone later in life, after I already had a child. But once I turned thirty-nine, I decided that there was no more time to lose.

I got the sperm-bank catalog in the mail. The donors were listed by race, height, coloring, and college major. There was an Irish-Italian one with curly blond hair and hazel eyes who studied religion and music. He was my top choice. And then number 3166, a philosophy major. He was six feet tall and of Portuguese-Hawaiian stock. I liked the idea of a good hybrid. I was avoiding German blood, a prejudice I've inherited from my mother. I thought it would depress me to pick out a man from a catalog, but I actually loved perusing the pages. No fuss and no muss. It was easy. We are living in a time when I could buy anything, including a father for my child. Every spare moment I flipped through the catalog, imagining my baby made practically all by myself, and savoring the freedom of not depending on one of those blind dates to be the man of my dreams. I could give myself a family. I'd have my techno-baby and then adopt a second one from Russia to complete my millennium-style family. I lay on the sofa and listened to the audiotapes I had ordered of several men who caught my fancy. I listened as they spoke of their goals, hobbies, families, and desire to travel. I listened carefully to the timbre of their voices to see who sounded kind and warm, and whittled the choice down. I called in to order longer profiles with information on their favorite pets, the type of music they liked, and medical histories for my top six choices.

"Number 3166?" I asked.

"Not available," said the voice on the line. How about 4255 or 8922? Not available on my first five choices. Men were allowed to donate sperm only a finite number of times so as not to flood the gene pool with their sperm. I couldn't believe I couldn't even *buy* the man of my dreams. I was going to have to settle for leftovers even at the sperm bank. The best ones had already been taken. But I was not deterred. Maybe it's better, I thought, if I use weaker genes and let mine dominate.

If I let myself, I sometimes got a little sad about resorting to this clinical, sterile approach to creating life. I hoped I could just sleep through the part where my gynecologist would squirt the purchased donor seed inside me. I wanted to be able to blank that part out. But mostly I took pleasure from having conquered my problem with men by reducing them to a vial of semen cooled by liquid nitrogen. Or maybe I was just angry with them because a good one hadn't shown up in time for me.

A baby tried to grow once ten years ago but I wasn't ready. He must have known that, so he lodged himself in my tube and never made the journey to my womb. The doctors told me it was just a bundle of cells caught in my fallopian tube. It was an ectopic pregnancy. There was no real fetus, they said. But I see him sometimes in my dreams. He is mangled, bloody, and crawling away from me. He is very real. He was wise enough to know it wasn't his time to enter the world. At the time I didn't want to bring a new life into such a messy life as mine. Now I hoped he would give me another chance.

I had been in California almost a year when my mother came to visit me. I expected it to be a repetition of the frustrations of hoping for and wanting a connection that rarely came. Of wanting her to ask about my life and love affairs and feelings, and the great emptiness that engulfed me when she didn't. When she couldn't. I didn't know if I would be able to tell her I was considering using a sperm bank to father her grandchild.

When I saw her tall, white-haired figure emerge from the crowded plane, I sensed it would be different this time. There was no big hug. She accepted my peck on the cheek, and I didn't feel dejected that she didn't embrace me; instead, I noticed the warmth in her pale blue eyes.

She rearranged my cooking utensils and sorted through my pots and pans. She tossed out some I had been carting around since college and bought me fancy new French cookware and linen napkins. She rearranged my furniture and organized my closets. She gave me what she knows how to give: her fine taste and knowledge of how things are supposed to be. We spent hours cutting damask and silk patches to choose a new fabric to cover my sofa, analyzing the merits of each one. I wished we could have had the same intensity in dissecting my life, but the home decorating felt like enough.

I noticed her hands and feet, slightly more wrinkled versions of my own. I remembered how those hands had lovingly brushed my tangled mop when I was a girl. Painstakingly, for what seemed like hours, she would unravel the knots. Never once, despite the bother, did she consider cutting it off. I was embarrassed by my hair; it was so wild and coarse and curly, nothing like all the other girls' thin, straight hair. My mother would always tell me it was my crowning glory. It was special, and it was OK to be different. She doesn't know how to use the words "I love you," but when she tells me never to cut my hair, or rearranges my closets, I feel her love and the irrelevance of those words and the hunger is gone.

During her visit she cooked nightly feasts for a parade of prospective suitors, which I considered a last-gasp attempt before I forged ahead at the sperm bank. She charmed them with her shrimp curry. Her pear tart and chiseled beauty were my best advertisement. When each one left on successive nights, she assessed their suitability. She watched closely how they treated Max. She made an effort, using her dog-breeding knowledge, to characterize their attributes. That one wasn't very well house-trained. This one wasn't very good breeding stock, not prepared to be a pack animal.

She tried to push me toward one particular suitor. He was smart, well traveled, and stable, but we were totally different. He liked ikebana flower arranging, a piece of wood with one bloom stuck in the middle. I preferred a big teapot stuffed with wildflowers. My furniture was big, carved, and curvy; his was angular, modern lines in black leather. I felt like a billowing Renaissance painting out of place in his austere modern Japanese living room with a single wall decoration of a bamboo stalk on rice paper; a baroque intruder at his tea party. I told her I felt nothing for him at all.

"That's ridiculous," she said. "You might grow to like him if you could appreciate all his good qualities."

"He said he would never let a dog sleep in the bed," I countered.

"Forget it. Get rid of him immediately," she said dismissively.

God forbid Max's needs shouldn't be met. My mother was trying to be more open with me about personal issues, but her priorities weren't going to change.

We spent each morning shoveling buttery croissants into our mouths at the bakery, sneering at the more typical California customers who were eating granola. Food snobbery and judging people by what they eat binds us together. I remember all the places we have eaten together: the time she took me to the UN delegates' dining room in New York as a little girl, or the Russian Tea Room. She wanted us to be comfortable with finer things, even if we didn't have them. She made it easy for me to sit comfortably at a dinner table with world leaders or in palaces or embassies and never be thrown by a place setting with five different knives and forks.

Over the years, I had spent so much time mourning what she couldn't give me that I didn't always appreciate all the things she could. I love her for all the lore she hands down to me, for all her refinement, for her enormous spirit and steadfastness in bringing us up almost entirely on her own, for her ability to not just survive, but to rise above the fray. I appreciate her emphasis on table manners and fine food and how to live life—always to use teacups with saucers, to set the table even if just for yourself. Her standards helped her survive, and I notice they have taken root in me. Her courage and strength are the greatest gifts she gave. They make up for whatever else is missing.

It is hard to paint a picture of my father in my mind. It is put together from the memories of a young girl and from fragments I collected later on from others who knew him. He had speckled hazel eyes and wore glasses. He was pale and freckled, except for his left forearm, which was often tanned from leaning it out the car window. I remember his rages. He would come home Sunday evening after a trip to his mother's, where he went most weekends.

He would sit at the table and first eat a bowl of cornflakes, then some scrambled eggs, and then have dinner. It was as if he needed to eat all three meals at once to somehow retrieve the time he hadn't been at home with us. We were wary when he was at home, never knowing when he might blow up and there would be a fight. I didn't know how to act around him. It was much easier when he wasn't there. All that mattered to me was my mother's happiness, and his presence never brought that. Sometimes he would reach out to me and want to be my friend, want to know what I was working on in school. Part of me wanted that. Most of me recoiled, worried it would offend my mother if I wasn't one hundred percent on her side. His storms and moods were not all of him. He became weary and bloated from the cells run amok in his lymph glands. Their rampant advance drove him home to know his girls while there was still time. He taught me how to drive in his wreck of a car—one in a long line of jalopies unfit for the road. He wanted to help with our homework, drive us to parties, know our friends, and enter our lives. But he was a stranger by then. He wanted to talk. He was in the ground twenty years before I was ready to listen.

My father died before I could get to know him. Only years later could I realize how he, like my mother, had enormous courage. How he had the strength to try to break free from the stranglehold of his home. I never knew exactly what happened in his family, but it was bad enough to drive my father's oldest brother to suicide, and to break Uncle Leon's spirit. My father tried to escape, going to medical school in Northern Ireland, where he met a beautiful woman and had children with her. It did not work out well when he came home, but at least he had tried.

My father's presence colored every move I made in life. I looked for him in all the men I met. I looked for him in Russia, and found part of him in Dima. I looked for him in Israel and in the Jewish men to whom I've been attracted. I traveled far in my search for him. I finally found him much closer to home, in the place I was most afraid to look, where he had been all along. In me.

I noticed him now in my green eyes and curly hair and in the way I cock an eyebrow when someone says something idiotic, and in how I sometimes play chicken with the gas tank, letting it run on empty. I welcomed him as part of me, no longer banished, even when I cut up a banana in a bowl of cereal. My mother is with me too. When I iron my tablecloths or linen napkins and refuse to buy paper ones, or gather strays to my dinner table, I feel her presence. Their feud is finally played out. They are no longer at war inside me. I am free to let them both inhabit me in peace.

I narrowed down my choice of donor sperm to number 3261. I would never know his name or what he looked like, only that he had blue eyes and dark curls. That he loved animals and cared about the planet. I liked his deep, soothing voice on the audiotape and bought a year's supply lest he sold out, and stored him away until I was ready for insemination. It was going to be my fortieth birthday present to myself.

A few days after my purchase, I got an e-mail message out of the blue that changed my life. It was from a man I'd never met.

Dear Siobhan,

Greetings from China, land of long-lost correspondents. My name is Shep. Even though you don't know me, I want to tell you a story.

Many years ago I found myself drawn as if by music to the voice of a CNN correspondent in Europe, your voice. When I bothered to look up from my keyboard and started paying atten-

tion, I noticed they were always good stories under your (wonderful) name. Always a strong, intelligent presence. So I allowed myself to become a big fan and only talk about you to whoever else was in the room whenever I saw you on the air. . . .

I read the message over and over. It warmed me with its straightforward honesty. Shep sounded gentle and romantic. I had had plenty of admirers write me over the years, but this one felt different. He felt like a fellow traveler, someone who knew a lot about me without even trying, because he had been on the same road. I liked that he wanted to tell me a story. Could it be that what he was telling was the beginning of our story?

Shep wrote that he was a correspondent for *The New York Times* in China. It turned out that he knew a friend of mine at CNN, who told him that the two of us would be a good match. He also knew a high school friend of mine, who had also remarked on the similarities of Shep's and my paths, traveling and working as journalists, him in China, me in Russia. It almost seemed like a cosmic rule of love: as soon as I stopped looking for a man, one came and found me.

I wrote him back right away. I tried to sound as friendly and warm as he had, and asked a few questions so that he'd be sure to write back. Maybe I was just dreaming to think that he might be my soul mate, but the least I wanted was a second message.

I woke up to a message from him the next day. It was even warmer than the first. I could feel this man in the writing, thoughtful and sensitive and humorous. I found myself thinking about him all day long, and wanted nothing more than to get the next message from him.

Within a week we spoke on the phone for the first time. I had been a little nervous about hearing his voice, since my expectations about him were racing ahead fast. But it was not awkward at all. I felt completely natural and at home with him, as though I were talking to an old friend. We talked for three hours. He was very curious about everything: my time off, my moving to California, what my house looked like, and about Max. I felt reluctant to hang up, even though it was the middle of the night by the time we did.

Within days Shep and I were talking on the phone several times a day. I didn't care that it meant calling China. I wanted to tell him about everything I did each day. Since we were calling each other on opposite sides of the world, my morning was his evening, and vice versa. Soon he was calling to wake me in my morning, and I was returning the favor. We never ran out of things to say. All the mental lists I had about necessary qualities in a man went out the window. I just wanted to learn about Shep, to accept him the way he was.

I felt myself growing close to Shep, even though I had not yet met him. He became a feeling within me, one I couldn't visualize, but that I could feel distinctly. I was afraid to confide in my friends about him, fearing they would say I was crazy to get so excited about a man I had not even seen a picture of. But I realized that Shep reawakened something in me that I had thought might be dead. He taught me that I still held out hope that I could find a soul mate.

Two weeks after our first message, Shep flew from Shanghai to Los Angeles. We arranged to meet just before sunset, at a beautiful park near my home in Santa Monica that overlooks the ocean. Max and I walked down together at the appointed time. It was one of those perfect southern California evenings, clear and cool. Even though I had no idea what Shep looked like, I didn't care. I felt as though I already knew him, knew his strength and his grace, his intelligence and his love of life. I felt my heart racing. I told myself that it was possible that things would not turn out as I hoped. But I also knew that I had never been so excited about meeting anyone in my entire life.

I saw him from a distance in the park. He was holding a sandalwood fan from China. He seemed to recognize me, and started walking toward me. I was surprised by his appearance. He seemed familiar. He was tall, with fair, woolly hair and green eyes. I realized that he and I looked alike. Intuitively, I felt as though he were a long-lost part of me, like my other half. The first thing he did was lean down to stroke Max. And then he laughed, noticing that we were wearing the same shoes, black clogs. We walked and we talked, and sometimes just stared at each other, learning each other's face. And then, after about half an hour, he took my hand in his as we crossed the street. And the moment he touched me, I knew.

Uncle Leon, I thought, your most ardent wish is going to come true.

Epilogue

Once I had Shep in my life, I felt as if I had everything. But it also created a dilemma: what to do about 3261, my donor sperm. I was so determined to try to have a baby soon, a voice in my head told me not to postpone my plans for insemination just because I had met a new man, no matter how wonderful he was. Lori and other friends warned me not to bring it up with Shep too early in our budding relationship. But I felt I was keeping a big secret from him, and had to get it off my chest even though I didn't know how he would react. A few days into our romance, I got up my courage and said to Shep, "I need to tell you about the other man in my life."

His face fell. I quickly got up out of bed and went into the closet and pulled out 3261 to introduce him to Shep. His hurt look dissolved into a big smile when he saw that his rival was confined to a test tube. I explained to him the plan I had set in motion before our meeting. "But you have me now; you don't need him," Shep said.

"But I haven't even known you a week," I said. He smiled again. "You know me better than you know him," he said as he grabbed me and pulled me back under the covers. Shep moved to California two months later, as soon as he could wrap up his affairs in China and negotiate time off from *The New York Times* to write his own book. From the day he arrived, I felt like we belonged together. Even our furniture was in harmony, his Chinese treasures easily blending with my Russian antiques. I remained in a state of wonder that Shep and I found each other at all. It seemed such an amazing act of Providence. We had been living on opposite sides of the world, and still found a way to meet. I asked him over and over what it was that had given him the courage to write me out of the blue, but all he could say was that he had good intuition, and that this was our fate. We married within the year.

We started planning a family immediately. I worked for the CNN bureau in Los Angeles for a while as I finished writing this book. But my life had changed. I had often wondered if there could be life after CNN, if anything could ever be as exciting again. Would a tamer life bore me? Who would I be, if not a CNN reporter? Now it felt as though it was time for me to find out, and I stopped working there. I began to discover that a new stage of life was awaiting me, a quieter, more stable life, a life with greater pleasure in small wonders. In my corner of southern California, the flora constantly surprises me with its vivid colors and sweet fragrances, and I hardly pass a single rose or jasmine without pausing to savor the scent. In my new life I treasure long walks by the beach, lazy afternoons reading, and evenings cooking dinner at home with Shep. I have time—and peace of mind—to write. I no longer jump when the phone rings, worrying as I used to that a crisis breaking in some foreign land will mean I have to drop everything and race out the door. I can read the newspaper in bed each morning peacefully, instead of frantically scanning it for a disaster that might disrupt my life. I've had enough traveling and adventure to last several lifetimes. Now I am on an entirely different kind of journey: one of love and intimacy and, I hope, impending motherhood.

Acknowledgments

I always knew I wanted to write a book. But only one person seemed to believe I actually could even before I believed it: Lori Farris. She has been a tremendous support, giving wise counsel and heavy doses of reality at every twist and turn. She has also been my memory, recalling details of my life I myself had long forgotten. Without Lori's friendship and love, my life would have been a lot harder, and writing this book impossible.

All the people in the book are real, although, in some cases, names and identities have been changed. My memory of events is imperfect, but this is how I saw things and felt them.

I am especially grateful to my sisters, Alexandra and Francesca, for their love and memories. They are my oldest friends; they helped me survive in the family trenches. I am also immensely grateful to my mother, for the gift of life and the strength to live it.

She worked miracles bringing us up, always teaching us that nothing was beyond our reach.

Writing this book brought me closer to my father and to my uncle Leon, whom I thank for sending me all those wonderful letters. I thank my stepfather, Tim, for sharing confidences on all those airport runs. I also want to thank Beverly Kitaen-Morse for teaching me about living more fully and helping me out of the trenches, both figuratively and literally. Without Toby Eady's belief that my life deserved a book, I might never have written it. Nancy Bacal and her Wednesday-morning writing group took me to places I never thought I could go. Leslie Linka Glatter, Ellen Basian, Stuart Sender, and Stephen Grynberg heroically waded through early drafts, giving great suggestions. Sara Faison, with her impeccable grammar and ruthless eye for dangling participles, went through the final draft.

A special thank-you to Jenny Minton, my editor, and Elizabeth Sheinkman, my agent, for their tenacity in getting this published, and to Lennie Goodings, my editor in London.

All the crews and producers I worked with at CNN are a part of this book, and I want to thank them all for being my family for so many years. And, of course, Max, who, sadly, died before publication, for being a loyal animal companion through some lonely years, and who sat at my feet through the writing of this book.

And finally a profound thank-you to Shep, for finding me from the other side of the world and for giving this book such a happy ending by marrying me even after he had read it. Not only did he not run away, he stayed around and edited and reedited the book, caring about it as if it were his own.